CITIZEN
CHRISTIANS

The Rights and Responsibilities of Dual Citizenship

Richard D. Land
& Louis A. Moore
Editors

BROADMAN
&HOLMAN
PUBLISHERS

Nashville, Tennessee

To the staff of the Southern Baptist Christian Life Commission and our Board of Trustees

© Copyright 1994 • Broadman & Holman Publishers
All Rights Reserved
4212-37
ISBN: 0-8054-1237-9

Dewey Decimal Classification: 323
Subject Heading: CITIZENSHIP // CHRISTIANITY AND POLITICS//
CHURCH AND SOCIAL PROBLEMS
Library of Congress Catalog Number: 93-6692
Printed in the United States of America

Library of Congress Cataloging-in-Publication Data

Citizen Christians / Richard D. Land and Louis A. Moore, Editors.
     p.   cm.
  ISBN 0-8054-1237-9
  1. Christianity and politics--Baptists--Congresses.
2. Christianity and politics--United States--Congresses. 3. Church
and state--Baptists--Congresses. 4. Church and state--United
States--Congresses. 5. Baptists--Doctrines--Congresses.
6. Southern Baptist Convention--Doctrines--Congresses. I. Land,
Richard D. II. Moore, Louis A., 1946-
BR115.P7C386 1993
261.7--dc20   93-6692
                                                                           CIP

Contributors

Chapter 1. Richard D. Land is Executive Director of the Southern Baptist Christian Life Commission in Nashville, Tennessee. He holds a B.A. degree from Princeton University, a Th.M. degree from New Orleans Baptist Theological Seminary, and the D.Phil. from Oxford University.

Chapter 2. Morris H. Chapman is president of the Executive Committee of the Southern Baptist Convention and immediate past president of the Southern Baptist Convention. He was president of the SBC Pastors' Conference in 1986. He received his B.A. degree from Mississippi College, his M.Div. and D.Min. degrees from Southwestern Baptist Theological Seminary, and the S.T.D. degree from Southwest Baptist University.

Chapter 3. H. Edwin Young is president of the Southern Baptist Convention and pastor of Second Baptist Church of Houston. He received his B.A. degree from Mississippi College, his B.D. degree from Southeastern Baptist Theological Seminary and honorary D.D. degrees from Furman University, Criswell College, Mississippi College, and Hannibal-LaGrange College.

Chapter 4. Lynn R. Buzzard is Associate Professor of Law and Director of the Church-State Resource Center at Campbell University School of Law in Buies Creek, North Carolina. He received his M.A.T. degree from Duke University, his M.Div. from Duke Divinity School, and the J.D. degree from DePaul University College of Law.

Chapters 5 and 6. Carl F.H. Henry, founding editor of *Christianity Today*, is a world-renowned theologian, author, and lecturer-at-large with Prison Ministries in Arlington, Virginia. He received his B.A. and M.A. degrees from Wheaton College, his B.D. and Th.D. degree from Northern Baptist Theological Seminary, and the Ph.D. from Boston University.

Chapter 7. Roy T. Edgemon is Director of the Discipleship Training and Family Development Department at the Baptist Sunday School Board in Nashville. He is a graduate of Midwestern University and Southwestern Baptist Theological Seminary.

Chapter 8. Cal Thomas is a syndicated columnist, author, TV commentator, and former TV news reporter who now lives in Manassas, Virginia.

Chapter 9. William J. Bennett is former U.S. Secretary of Education and currently codirector of Empower America, a Distinguished Fellow at the Cultural Policy Studies at the Heritage Foundation, and a senior editor of *National Review* magazine. He served as director of the Office of National Drug Control Policy ("drug czar") from March 1989 to November 1990. He holds a B.A. degree from Williams College, a doctorate from the University of Texas, and a law degree from Harvard University.

Chapter 10. Beverly LaHaye is founder and president of Concerned Women for America and an author, speaker, and activist in Washington, D.C. She is the author of seven books and has been a weekly commentator on women's issues for UPI's Religion Service.

Chapter 11. H. Robert Showers, Jr., is Chief of the Commercial and Civil Litigation Section for the Gammon & Grange Law Firm in Washington, D.C. and former Executive Director of the National Obscenity Enforcement Unit in the Criminal Division of the United States Department of Justice in Washington. He received his J.D. degree from Wake Forest University School of Law.

Chapter 12. Jay Strack is an evangelist and author from Dallas. He has preached throughout the United States and in Israel, the former Soviet Union, England, China, and at various places in the Orient. He received his B.A. degree from Charleston Southern University, and his M.Div. and D. Min. degrees from Luther Rice Seminary. He also attended Southwestern Baptist Theological Seminary.

General editor Louis A. Moore is Director of Media and Products for the SBC Christian Life Commission. He received his B.A. from Baylor University and his M.Div. from Southern Baptist Theological Seminary.

Preface

We Christians are citizens of two realms—the earthly and spiritual. Such dual citizenship includes rights and responsibilities in both spheres.

But which comes first? Jesus said we are to "render unto Caesar those things that are Caesar's and unto God those things that are God's." Throughout the Bible, we are reminded that our primary focus must be on God and that which is of God. The apostle Paul tells us Christians that we are to support the civil government unless the authorities require us to support or to do evil in direct contradiction to our ultimate allegiance to our Heavenly Father.

We chose the title for this book to illustrate the proper biblical order for Christians wrestling with the issues involved in being citizens of both realms. We are Christians first; at the core of our being should be our dedication to God through our Lord and Savior Jesus Christ. But we are also citizens of the state.

Grammatically, Christian is our subject, our basis. Citizen is our adjective; it modifies and explains further who we are. Our citizenship modifies our Christianity. It is certainly not the other way around. We are not citizens first, then Christians.

We compiled this book to stimulate Christian thinking about pressing needs in understanding this dual citizenship. Throughout the world today, new governments are searching for answers to the balance between the spiritual and earthly. In our own country, the highest courts in the land continue to wrestle with many of these same issues.

This book originated in discussions surrounding the Southern Baptist Christian Life Commission's 25th Annual

Seminar in Washington, D.C., in March 1992. It grew out of a belief both at the Christian Life Commission and Broadman Press that serious Christians want to know more about the issues contained on these pages.

Special thanks go to Edith Wilson, the CLC's editorial assistant; Lee Hollaway, who painstakingly checked the manuscripts for accuracy; and Trent Butler and John Landers of Broadman for their guidance throughout the project.

We pray that God will use this book to help enlighten Southern Baptists as well as non-Southern Baptists about the proper biblical balance for Citizen Christians.

Richard D. Land and Louis A. Moore

Contents

Introduction

By Richard D. Land and Louis A. Moore

This volume originated from the 25th Annual Seminar of the Southern Baptist Christian Life Commission, held in Washington, D.C., in March 1992. The Christian Life Commission staff designed the seminar, entitled "Citizen Christians: Their Rights and Responsibilities," to contribute to the ongoing discussion among Southern Baptists about what it means for Christians to be citizens of two realms—the earthly and the spiritual.

The seminar was designed to address such issues as: What does the Bible say the Christian's attitude ought to be toward the state in which he or she lives? What does the term "separation of church and state" mean in our culture today? How can Christians make an impact on their governments? What is the future of religion in politics? What exactly can a Christian do in politics that is moral, legal, and respectable?

We were mindful that we held the seminar during a year in which Americans once again were going to the polls to select a President and Vice President for the next four years. But we were also eager to design a seminar that answered questions that extended far beyond the 1992 elections. Questions that pertain to the election process and what role Christians should and can play in it are far greater than just the issues of one particular campaign.

The seminar's logo reflected the position from which the topics were presented. The logo depicted an open Bible as the foundation with the *Declaration of Independence* behind and

1

above it. We believe many of the guiding principles on which our own nation was formed were derived from the Bible. The *Declaration of Independence* particularly reflects an understanding of God's principles found in the Bible.

The apostle Paul instructs us that as Christians we have the responsibility to be good citizens of the state "for conscience sake" because God has ordained government to punish and restrict evil-doers and to reward and protect moral behavior (Rom. 13:1-7). Christians are to support the civil government unless the authorities require a believer to support or to do evil in direct contradiction to their ultimate allegiance to their Heavenly Father.

The Bible says (John 19:14; 1 Cor. 5:9-10) that Christians are to be *in* the world but not *of* the world. The Bible also says (Matt. 5:13-16) society is to be transformed by the Christian's witness, influence, and presence.

In His Sermon on the Mount, Jesus gave the New Testament church part of its marching orders. He said (Matt. 5:13-16) that we are to be salt and light in a decadent world. A detailed exegesis of these verses shows that in the New Testament era salt was a preservative and disinfectant. Salt cannot preserve unless it touches that which it is to preserve. Likewise, light cannot illuminate and expose unless it is taken to the area that is to be illuminated. We are to be God's salt and light in the world, preserving and illuminating.

These passages clearly indicate we Southern Baptists should not be monastics who live apart from the world in a monastery set high on a hill. The responsibilities of citizen Christians include not just obedience to the state but involvement in society.

The present chapters have, in the process of being adapted from an oral presentation format, been edited and reorganized into subject groups. The first three chapters are introductory. Christian Life Commission Executive Director Richard D. Land begins by producing an overview on the issue of "Citizen Christians Have Rights Too." He attempts to answer the questions about who citizen Christians are, why their first allegiance is to God, and what their rights and responsibilities are in the political process.

Additionally, Southern Baptist Executive Committee President Morris H. Chapman addresses how important it is for Southern Baptists to follow Jesus' admonition to be salt and light and applies it to the political process.

2

Then Southern Baptist Convention President H. Edwin Young offers a biblical explanation for the role of the Christian in the state and in the political process. He defines leadership in terms of a leader's ability to lead and lifts up Nehemiah as an example of a God-fearing leader.

The next section falls under the subheading of "Defining Separation of Church and State." Lynn R. Buzzard, associate professor of law and director of the Church-State Resource Center at the Campbell University School of Law in Buies Creek, N.C., focuses attention on what the U.S. Constitution really says about the phrase that is not in the Constitution but which has come to characterize the First Amendment—"the separation of church and state." He offers some intriguing critiques of current issues regarding "separation." Noted theologian and author Carl F.H. Henry, founding editor of *Christianity Today*, then addresses the topic, "The Uneasy Conscience of Modern Fundamentalism: 45 Years Later." He sketches the move of conservative Christians from outside the political process to the development of an important voice in American society and politics today.

The section titled "Issues Looming on the Horizon" is forward-looking in its perspective. Dr. Henry brings to bear his years of experience in writing and speaking on church-state separation when he addresses the topic "Religious Liberty as a Cause Celebre." Roy T. Edgemon, director of the Discipleship and Family Development Division at the Baptist Sunday School Board and a popular interim pastor of numerous churches in the southeastern United States, wrote the chapter "Reacting to the Needs of the Nation," in which he discusses how a Christian's pilgrimage and spiritual growth are intertwined with civic responsibilities.

Two prominent national leaders conclude this third section with an intriguing look at the issue from outside the Southern Baptist Convention. Nationally syndicated columnist Cal Thomas, whose provocative columns and TV commentary reflect his evangelical Christian beliefs, challenges Christians to retain their biblical perspective while impacting society at large. Then former federal drug czar William J. Bennett, now codirector of Empower America, a distinguished fellow at the Heritage Foundation and a senior editor of *National Review* magazine, offers insight into how changing cultural norms in American society and wrong ideals led to the current moral crisis in which drugs and sexual immorality abound.

The last section, "Practical Application," begins with a provocative article by Beverly LaHaye, founder and president of Concerned Women for America and an author, speaker, and activist in Washington, D.C., entitled "How Christians Make an Impact on Their Government." She details ways that Christians can, by understanding the political process, make a determinable impact on the various levels of American government.

Then H. Robert Showers, Jr., chief of the Commercial and Civil Litigation Section for the Gammon & Grange Law Firm in Washington, D.C., and former executive director of the National Obscenity Enforcement Unit in the Criminal Division of the U.S. Department of Justice, shares how Christians can make a difference by working inside the government. He tells of his own experiences trying to help stamp out pornography, particularly child pornography, in this country through his efforts in the Department of Justice.

Evangelist Jay Strack, a member of the National Drug Control Policy Task Force now headed by drug czar Robert Martinez, concludes our presentation with a moving chapter on "How Christians Can Have an Impact as Volunteers." He tells about how he and others have made an impact on society by following the teaching of Jesus in modern-day life.

Together, these 12 speakers describe the many ways Christians, following the leadership of the Lord Jesus Christ, can impact our society, culture, and political system.

PART I

What Does It Mean to Be a Citizen Christian?

1

Citizen Christians
Have Rights Too

By Richard D. Land

The New Testament teaches us that Christians are citizens of two realms—the earthly and the spiritual—and they have *rights* and *responsibilities* in both spheres. I have been asked the question several times since we produced the tract entitled "Citizen Christians: Their Rights and Responsibilities," which was the lead-in to the theme of this conference, "Why Citizen Christians and not Christian Citizens?" The answer is that we did that purposely, deliberately, and with much forethought. We wanted to put the emphasis on the noun. We are Christians, and the adjective "citizen" is to modify the noun "Christian," and not the other way around. We are Christians first, foremost, and always.

Our involvement, our attempts to make a difference are because we are Christians and because we have responsibilities both in the realm of the nation and in the realm of our Lord's Kingdom. We have responsibilities and we have rights, and those responsibilities and rights are in both realms. As citizens of heaven, which is what we are called in Philippians 3:20, we as believers are commanded to be obedient to the

Lord Jesus (Ex. 20:1-5). Our Lord's instruction to "render therefore unto Caesar the things which be Caesar's and unto God the things which be God's" (Luke 20:25) means that we must give ultimate allegiance to God. Rendering unto Caesar the things that are Caesar's means that we pay our taxes, but it also means a lot more. The apostle Paul instructs us that as Christians we have the responsibility to be good citizens "for conscience' sake" because God has ordained government to punish and restrict evildoers and to reward and to protect moral behavior (Rom. 13:1-7). We are to support the civil government unless its authorities require us to support or do that which is in direct contradiction to our ultimate allegiance to our Heavenly Father.

Jesus Commands Us to Be "Salt"and "Light"

We are also commanded by our Lord and Savior Jesus Christ, who gives us our ultimate marching orders, to be the "salt" of the earth and the "light" of the world. This means that Christians as citizens are to be in active engagement with the world, preserving as salt and illuminating as light. So our responsibilities as Citizen Christians include not just *obedience* to the state but *involvement* in society. That should not be a radical notion if we correctly understand our heritage as Baptists.

The *Baptist Faith and Message,* our confession of faith, affirms this call to involvement with the world when it states under "The Christian and the Social Order" that "every Christian is under obligation to seek to make the will of Christ supreme in his own life and in human society." The confession says that Christians not only "should oppose, in the spirit of Christ, every form of greed, selfishness, and vice," but "should seek to bring industry, government, and society as a whole under the sway of the principles of righteousness, truth, and brotherly love."

This statement by our forebears clarifies our *responsibilities* as Christians and our *rights* as citizens. When we bring our religious and moral convictions and our faith affirmations into the public marketplace of ideas and involve ourselves in the social and political arena, we are standing solidly within the best of our traditions as Americans and as Baptists. Far too often in recent decades we have allowed misunderstandings and misleading applications of church/state separation and religious liberty to be twisted into a meaning which was never intended by those who pioneered those principles. That

7

twisted understanding is that if we have our convictions, if we have our beliefs because of our faith understanding, then somehow we are disqualified from the public marketplace of ideas. Often we hear it under the myth, "Well, you know you can't legislate morality."

Yes, We Can Legislate Morality

It is a myth to say that you can't legislate morality. Nothing could be more false. As a practical matter, all governments legislate morality. Laws against murder, laws against theft, and laws against rape are the legislation of morality. And when we as civilized societies pass laws against murder, theft, and rape, we are not so much seeking to impose our morality on murderers and thieves and rapists as we are seeking to keep them from imposing their immorality on their victims.

In Romans 13, the longest sustained New Testament statement on the Christian and his or her relationship to the civil government and the purpose of civil government, the apostle Paul says that God ordained the civil magistrate to punish those who do that which is wrong and to reward those who do good. If we say that people of faith are disqualified from the discussion and the definition of what is good and what is evil, then we have allowed ourselves to be led by moral pygmies whose moral compass is askew. We have a right and a responsibility to be involved.

It is impossible to understand American history from the beginning until now if you try to understand it under a rubric of separation of church and state which does not allow people of faith conviction to bring those convictions into the public marketplace. There would never have been an abolitionist movement without people of faith. There would never have been a child labor reform movement without people of faith. There would never have been a civil rights movement without people of faith. Virtually every major movement to right an injustice or a wrong in our society throughout our long history has been undergirded and sustained by people of religious faith.

Christians Have Rights
and Responsibilities in Society

Roger Williams, the great symbol of separation of church and state, preached against a state church. Yes, he preached for a separate entity for the church. Yes, he said that people should be free to worship or not to worship. But when they got around to writing the indictment against him for which they were going to arrest him and put him in chains and send him back to England, do you know what the first item against him was? That he was saying that the colonists didn't own the land because they received it by patent from the king and didn't pay the Indians for it. Thus, Williams asserted it still belonged to the Indians. Roger Williams, the champion of separation of church and state, was up to his colonial eyebrows in the most perplexing and difficult moral issue of his day—the colonial mistreatment of the Native Americans. He didn't understand separation of church and state to mean that people of religious faith were to be moved aside and segregated in a type of "philo-sophical apartheid" from the debate of what was right and what was wrong in society. Clearly, as Americans we have a *right* and as Christians we have a *responsibility* to be involved in the moral debates about right and wrong in our society.

Jesus says in John 8:32 that we "shall know the truth, and the truth shall make [us] free." The task of the Christian does not end when he or she discovers truth. He is commis-sioned to take that truth into the world and proclaim it. Few Christians have been called to live in a more exciting time than the one in which we now live.

Recently I was in a consultation on abortion in Princeton, New Jersey. We spent some time discussing what previous era would be similar to our situation in America in 1992. Is it like the situation in the eighteenth century, when people were openly talking about the demise of the Christian faith in the Western world before the great evangelical revivals? Is our sit-uation analogous to the first century, when Christianity invaded and ultimately penetrated and overcame a pagan and an idolatrous culture? The conclusion that some of us reached is that we are in worse shape than either one. It is not like the eighteenth century; it is not even like the first century, because in the first century they attempted to invade, penetrate, and convert a pre-Christian culture. We are trying to bring back a "post-Christian culture" which has heard the truth and has rejected it, often within as well as without the walls of local churches and other supposed repositories of reli-gious truth.

Having discerned the truth, we have an obligation "to be always ready to give a reasonable explanation of the hope that lies within us" (1 Pet. 3:15). As John Stott has observed,

9

It is comparatively easy to be faithful if we do not care about being contemporary, and easy also to be contemporary if we do not bother to be faithful. It is the search for a combination of truth and relevance which is exacting. Yet nothing else can save us from an insensitive loyalty to formulae and shibboleths on the one hand, and from a treasonable disloyalty to the revelation of God on the other.[1]

Our Responsibility Is "Both/And"

It never has been and never will be accurate for Christians to debate our responsibility either to be a witness *or* to be salt and light. It always has been and always will be "both/and." We are disloyal to our Savior if we neglect evangelism, and we deny the incarnation of our Savior, "the Word made flesh," if we see the flesh, that real world of human beings, as secondary or irrelevant. We must do both. It is blasphemous to seek to feed the hungry and not tell them about the Bread of Life. It is blasphemous to seek to clothe the naked and not tell them about the whole armor of God. It is blasphemous to seek to house the homeless and not tell them that in our Father's house are many mansions. It denies the incarnation to preach the gospel of light without being also the salt that preserves and the light that penetrates the darkness.

We Must Tell The Whole Truth

In our involvement as citizens, which is our right and which is our responsibility, we must remember, as William Bennett so eloquently and succinctly put it in a meeting I attended at the White House in 1991, that "We are the government. We have to be the government. You are the church. Be the church." We must tell the whole truth. And we must remember, as John Killinger wrote:

> In the end, it is the miracle of preaching, the magic of the gospel, that dispels the gloom again from this much-miracled, time-wearied Camelot of ours, and sets its knights and ladies all adance again. . . . It is the supreme gift of God to this soul spent, jag-jaded age we live in.[2]

Amen.

Notes

1. John Stott, *Christian Mission in the Modern World* (Downers Grove: InterVarsity Press, 1976), 43.
2. John Killinger, *The Centrality of Preaching in the Total Task of Ministry* (Waco,Tx.: Word, 1969), 85-86.

2

Kneel Down and Be Counted

By Morris H. Chapman

As I prepared to allow my name to be placed in nomination for president of the Southern Baptist Convention in 1990, God laid upon my heart a reminder that America is in a spiritual and moral crisis, desperately needing to hear a word from God. Before my election, which was by no means assured, my good friends had fear in their eyes, but I had a peace that it was God's will for me to allow my name to be placed in nomination, whatever the result. In light of that sense of God's leadership, I felt the Lord speaking to my heart saying, "I want you to do everything possible if you're elected to speak about the need for spiritual awakening and revival in this country."

So after I was elected and we began preparing for our 1991 Convention in Atlanta, I called our Southern Baptist people to pray for spiritual awakening in America. We can't manufacture renewal. It is not something we work to achieve. It is something for which we must pray. I rejoiced on that Wednesday night of the 1991 Convention when I looked out across that audience of 25,000. In the midst of that evening of

11

prayer for spiritual awakening I watched tears fall from the eyes of my brothers and sisters in Christ. I, too, was caught up in the moment and found those same tears coming to my eyes. I praised the Lord for that very stirring moment of inspiration.

As I left the Convention, my question to the Lord was "Oh God, what do we do now? I know that building your Kingdom on this earth is something more than this one-moment experience." I felt the Lord impressing me to reach out to call upon us, person by person and church by church, to begin praying.

God Points to a Prayer-Chain Ministry

The Lord led me to a model prayer ministry at the First Baptist Church of Merritt Island, Florida. It was put together by Larry Thompson, who is now at the Dauphin Way Baptist Church in Mobile, Alabama. I believe that God was telling me to take that model and call all Southern Baptists to pray, church by church, somewhat like a prayer chain. We have called it the Watchman National Prayer Alert. Dr. Jimmy Draper and members of the Baptist Sunday School Board, especially the leadership of Discipleship Training, Dr. Roy Edgemon, and others, are working to see that the mechanics of this proposal are put in place. The Baptist Sunday School Board has allocated thousands of dollars for this project.

I appointed Larry Thompson as chairman of the Watchman National Prayer Alert, and we began to send out a call to all Southern Baptist churches to begin praying. I felt God leading me to ask Southern Baptists to pray for Him to first build a hedge of protection around our beloved Southern Baptist Convention, and second that the devil wouldn't get in, but we would get out and beyond that hedge to reach our world for Christ.

By March 1992 more than 1,700 churches had requested to be assigned to an hour a week to pray. There are 168 hours in each week, so that means that more than ten churches are praying each hour of each week for this revival. Already God is beginning to do some phenomenal things. I hope you will join me in praying that church after church will continue to get involved in the Watchman National Prayer Alert.

Prayer must underwrite everything we accomplish in this nation. I am not an ethicist. I am a preacher of the Word of God who has upon his heart the need for spiritual awakening in America and the need to pray for God to so move and stir the hearts of Southern Baptists that this spiritual awakening would come to us and, thus, through us to this nation.

However, if the spark of revival begins somewhere outside our denominational boundaries, I trust God will give us the grace to run after it and be a part of it.

America Is in Need of Revival

We are talking about a mammoth responsibility of being Christian in America today. There is much right with this country. There is little doubt about it. I would rather live in America than anywhere in all the world, and God has given me the privilege to travel in other parts of the world. There are those good things about each nation which we are drawn to, but I am always glad to come home to these United States of America. I can say, "There's no place like home." However, that does not mean that we are never in need of a housecleaning when we come home. Things get dusty, sometimes downright dirty.

In Acts, Peter and John stood before the rulers of the day, who questioned them, "By what power, or by what name, have ye done this?" (4:7). Notice in Acts 4:13, "Now when they saw the boldness of Peter and John, and perceived that they were unlearned and ignorant men, they marvelled; and they took knowledge of them, that they had been with Jesus." There is no premium on ignorance in this verse, but it means these men were unlettered; that is, they had not had formal education. There was a power about them that mystified the rulers in Jerusalem: "They took knowledge of them, that they had been with Jesus."

No National Revival in Over 85 Years

We have not had national revival in this country for over 85 years. In fact, it has been over 130 years since we have had revival which ignited within these shores. Over 85 years ago we experienced a national revival which swept this country like a prairie fire. It was the aftermath of the Welsh revival, which began, in my understanding, one night when a young girl in a small church in the midst of a testimonial meeting stood up to say, "I love the Lord Jesus Christ with all my heart." So simple as to be profound. Stirred by the Holy Spirit of God, the congregation was electrified. Repentance came to the hearts of the people. They were kneeling at the altar, praying, some coming to know Christ as Savior, and others renewing their covenant with God. Revival swept from church to church and across that nation and came to America.

There were those who doubted. They were the skeptics who said, "Well, those who are being saved will not stay saved. It is fleeting. It is all a flash in the pan." And, in a way, they were right. After five years, only 80,000 of the 100,000 were still faithfully walking in Christ.

In the midst of all of that, God had been leading a man to attend prayer meeting for 11 or 12 years. We know that man in history by the name of Evan Roberts. There were many times when he thought about pulling out, but again and again God turned him away from the crowd and the streets and brought him to those prayer meetings. During one of those morning meetings, the evangelist pleaded that the Lord would bend the people. The Spirit got a hold on this Evan Roberts, and God said to him, "That's what you need. You need to be bent." Here is my interpretation of how Roberts began to describe his experience:

"I felt a living force coming into my bosom. This grew and grew, and I was almost bursting. What boiled in me was that verse God commending His love. I fell on my knees and with my arms on the seat in front of me, the tears and perspiration flowed freely. I thought blood was gushing forth. Certain friends approached me to wipe my face. Meanwhile, I was crying out, 'Oh, Lord, bend me, bend me,' and then suddenly the glory broke. After I was bent, a wave of peace came over me, and the audience sang, 'I Hear Thy Welcome Voice.' As they sang, I thought of the Judgment Day, and I was filled with compassion with those that would have to bend on that day, and I wept. Henceforth, the salvation of souls became the burden of my heart, and from that day I was on fire with the desire to go through the country of Wales, and if it were possible, to even pay God for the privilege of going."

From that point on, the young man of 26 years of age went everywhere spreading the fires of revival. The chapels were thronged, with hundreds more outside. At his appearance often there would be religious fervor and excitement and, with a few words of exhortation or a brief prayer, it would often suffice to set the congregation ablaze, and the people would burst into singing and then give testimony followed by prayer and singing again. Indeed, it was said that all of Wales was like a praise meeting. Mealtimes and other routine practices were neglected and forgotten, and God moved throughout the whole principality in saving and in purifying power. Heaven-sent revival truly visited those people in that country.[1]

The point of the story is that in the midst of it all there was a man who began to pray, "Lord, bend me."

I have tried to be faithful through the years to speak without fear and with conviction the truth of God's Holy Word, and I believe that today as never before there is a responsibility incumbent upon us to speak about the issues which are degrading our land and tearing us apart. I applaud those of you whose primary calling in life is to hold the issues up against the Bible and say, "Wait a minute. This is wrong," or, "Yes, this is right." But if, in fact, we shall be the success God would have us to be, we must stand four-square on those issues only after having knelt and known the face, heart, and mind of God. May God help us neither to strike out, nor to speak what we speak without being empowered by the Holy Spirit of God, whether we preach from the pulpit of the local church or whether we sit to testify in Congress.

God's Anointing Is Imperative

Our words become empty sounds, clanging cymbals, if, in fact, they do not come with the anointing of the Spirit of God. It is important not only to be anointed by God's Spirit in the pulpit and in the halls of Congress, but in our everyday walk, in every word we say. In fact, our nation will be changed more rapidly by what is said in the streets than by what is said in the pulpits of the land. Why? Because so much of our nation's population has ceased to come hear us in the pulpits. In fact, my greatest opportunity (and it would be so for most every pastor) to teach about salvation to the lost population is in a funeral service. Oh, I don't preach with a boisterousness that would be inappropriate in that setting, but I want to tell you, when you conduct that funeral service, people are listening.

The African antelope called the gnu has an interesting characteristic. When attacked, the gnu kneels and returns the attack from its knees. That is a great lesson for all of us. We can only overcome those who hinder the work of God by going to God in prayer. Unless we do, there is no power, no driving force.

In Acts 4, as Peter and John were released, they went among those of their own company. There was a prayer meeting, and in verse 24 they began with the word *Lord*, and in verse 30 they ended with the word *Jesus*. All, through praying, come to God the Father in the name of Jesus Christ our Lord.

15

The Bible says in Acts 4:31, "And when they had prayed, the place was shaken where they were assembled together." They were united in prayer, and prayer brings power. The power of prayer shook this early church and did something to these disciples. They were filled with the Holy Spirit. They covenanted together to pray. When the members will praise the Lord and fervently pray for power, God will anoint that congregation with supernatural power.

People today make fun of Jonathan Edwards's sermon, "Sinners in the Hands of an Angry God." It was said that when he preached that message, men held on to the pillars of the building to keep from slipping into hell. There are those who say that's just an illustration of Puritan extremism, but most people who make fun of Jonathan Edwards's sermon do not know what went on before he preached that sermon. He did not eat or sleep for three days and three nights before he stood to preach, and he prayed this prayer: "Oh, God, give me New England. Oh, God, give me New England." When he rose to preach, those who saw him said it looked as if he had been staring straight into the face of God. It's no wonder that when he preached, many felt convicted of their need to be saved, and revival shook New England.[2]

You might say the prayer meeting in Acts 4 was only a prayer meeting. It was only a prayer meeting that Jonathan Edwards had. It was only a haystack prayer meeting where the modern missions movement was born. It was only a prayer meeting, yet from that college prayer group, the Methodist church was brought into existence. It was only from a New York City storefront prayer meeting that a revival swept America.

When we go to do what we do, let us go in prayer. Let us not forget that when we stand to speak on the issues, God may give us the opportunity to lead others to Jesus Christ. Our work is incomplete if we simply stand on the issues and forget that some who hear us are in desperate need of the Savior. God help us to tell them why we believe as we do, for they need to hear that as they hear what it is we believe.

According to the Book of Daniel, Nebuchadnezzar, the king of Babylon, laid siege to Jerusalem. He had a disregard for the things of God. The Bible says in Daniel 1:1 that he had a disrespect for the purpose of God. Jerusalem represented all that God stood for in the world. God pitched His tent in Jerusalem, but Nebuchadnezzar was so unconcerned that he came up against Jerusalem. He was one who disrespected the purpose of

God. He disrespected the place of God. He went right into the house of God. He desecrated the holy vessels and carried them to the house of his own gods. Nothing was sacred or holy. It is tragic when we have nothing left that is holy.

Nebuchadnezzar had a disrespect for the people of God and captured the children of the nobility. He seized the leadership of Judah. He had a plan to win the allegiance of the brilliant local youth. He determined to win them through education and training. He sought to confuse them. He removed from them every outward evidence of God. Notice the first thing he did. He changed their names. There was Daniel, which means "God has judged"; Hananiah, "Jehovah is gracious"; Mishael, "Who is God"; and Azariah, which means "Jehovah has helped." They were renamed after the Babylonian gods: Belteshazzar, Shadrach, Meshach, and Abednego.

Nebuchadnezzar taught them the philosophy and language of the pagans. He attempted to lead them to develop compromising attitudes. Now there was nothing wrong with the food at the king's table except that all of it was against the Levitical law under which they had been trained. It was good food, pleasing to the taste. The king took the necessary time to accomplish his purpose—three years. Those who would undermine this nation know that their only hope is in the educational process of our young people. He wanted to reduce the individual to one of many, causing them to lose their identities. He sought to cause them to compromise. What was his purpose? He wanted to serve his own selfish interests, to turn these young men from God to the lesser ways and lower purposes in life.

We, today, are not in Babylon, but Babylon is in us. In America, we are experiencing an outburst of moral decadence that defies all rhyme and reason. If we ever are defeated as a nation, it will not be for the lack of military defense, but rather for the lack of moral defense.

Principally, in our nation, the religion that would undermine Christianity is secular humanism. Many of us believe the Supreme Court, starting in 1962, began to define secular humanism as a nontheistic religion. That trend began with the *Engel* v. *Vitale* case in 1962 and the *Abington School District* v. *Schempp* case in 1963. The Bible warns us against such religions in Proverbs 14:12: "There is a way which seemeth right unto a man, but the end thereof are the ways of death." Secular humanism and atheism are opposite sides of the same coin. Atheism says, "I don't believe in God." Secular humanism says,

17

"I believe in man to the exclusion of God." Those who brought secular humanism to America knew that atheism would not sell readily, so they disguised it as secular humanism: "I believe in man to the exclusion of God." It teaches that there is no authority, no absolute. Humanism denies the sovereignty of God and the Lordship of Jesus Christ. The absolutes of God's Word are being dissolved and watered down until persons are left with no convictions, no courage, and nothing but compromise. Humanistic thinking has given birth to situation ethics, doing what seems to be right to the individual in a given situation. God is a God of absolutes, yet humanistic teachers try to instill in the minds of our young people that there is no authority but themselves, not God and not their parents.

It Is Not Too Late

What hope is there? Is it too late to change course and preserve the freedoms we have cherished in this greatest nation on earth? There is a way, and that way is the way of faith by conviction. Out of the heart flow the issues of life (Prov. 4:23).

What can be done in faith? Here is what Daniel did. He determined a course of action that would not defile him. He was probably ridiculed when he resisted the food, but he stated his case objectively, clearly, and firmly, but not rudely. Not only was he a man of conviction, but he was a man of courage. He gained respect. Persons have always had respect for one who believes something. It has been said that we have developed in this nation preachers who have learned the art of almost saying something. Persons always have respect for you if you believe something.

A person of faith does not waste time on indecision. Neither did Daniel or his friends. They didn't hold a stockholder's meeting to decide what to do. They already, by faith, knew and understood God's purpose. There is nothing to lose and everything to gain by faith. They were persons of decision who were willing to say, "Here I stand."

Stand Tall on Our Knees

So, we are to kneel down and be counted. We are to stand tall on our knees. Yes, we are to stand, but when we stand we must know we have been with God. Before we talk to others about God we need to talk to God about them. We need to pray for those who would oppose the truth of God's Holy Word.

John Knox, the great preacher, said that he feared God so very much that he never feared the face of anyone else. He declared, "A man with God is always in the majority."3 Martin Luther said, "Here I stand—I cannot do otherwise. God help me."4 Athanasius, one of the church fathers, took his stand, "against the world." When a man is loyal to Christ, he is free. Therein is his only true freedom.

Speaking of courage, there was a rural preacher who once prayed, "Lord, give me a backbone as big as a sawlog and ribs like the sleepers under the church floor. Put iron shoes on me and galvanized britches. Give me a rhinoceros hide for skin, and hang a wagonload of determination up in the gable ends of my soul. Help me to sign a contract to fight the devil as long as I've got a fist and then bite him as long as I've got a tooth and then gum him until he dies."

The Declaration of Independence contains 1,321 words and takes about eight minutes to read. Those who signed it knew that by doing so they were putting their lives and property in jeopardy. Had England prevailed, they could have been put to death for treason. As it was, there were times during the war when they had to flee for their lives, and some had their homes vandalized or destroyed. It is said that the reason John Hancock wrote his name so large on the document was to make sure King George could not miss it. Hancock was committed to pay the price of liberty.

Much is being said today about the economy and about bondage. I had the privilege of having a Romanian pastor stand in my pulpit. Here are some of the things he said:

> Bondage is not a term that sticks with geography only. Bondage was the problem of human life having absolutely no value. We were just spare parts. We were just figures in a faceless machine that was always ready to replace any one of us. The thing that we realized in Romania was the fact that we were actually living our lives exchanging obedience for food. We were in a position in which the main religion in Romania was not Eastern Orthodoxy, as they still believe; it was survival. Everybody was worshiping the daily bread. Very often in our country people have asked, "How will things change?" and some believe the change will come from perestroika.
>
> By the way, do you know what perestroika is? They said in the newspapers in our country after the revolution, when finally we regained our consciousness and started speaking, they said they did not understand it either in the

Soviet Union. So one day a poor woman who had a son in the city working in a factory invited him home and said,

"Son, what is this thing called perestroika? Would you be so kind as to explain it to me?"

So the son looked around and he saw two buckets. One was filled with pebbles. The other was empty. He grabbed the one that was full and emptied the pebbles into the other bucket. And so he said, "Mom, this is perestroika."

"Well, son, I still don't understand. It is still an empty bucket and still a full one."

"Yes, Mother, but haven't you heard the noise?"

We hoped that would bring freedom, but it did not. But just as the Israelites sent 70 people to bring some food from Egypt, they stayed a bit too long there, and actually they ended up belonging there, while their place and their calling was not at all in the land of Egypt. Their calling was somewhere in the promised land, lifting up God's testimony, not there making bricks for Pharaoh, but that's exactly how we ended up in this kind of bondage. We thought that if today there is freedom that is taken away from us, if tomorrow another freedom is taken away from us, if the next day they will close a church and the day after they will put in prison one of our very good Christian leaders, it will be all right. We still had something to eat. But when we ended up in bondage, we had nothing.

It was your Benjamin Franklin—and let me tell you, our Benjamin Franklin as well, because his quotes were moved under the counter from one colleague of mine to another, and we were reading in secret his words—who said, 'Whoever renounces the basic liberties for some security doesn't deserve either one.' That is something that comes from you, and we have ended up exactly like that—no freedom, no security, for where your fear starts, your freedom stops. We have lived for years and years and years destroying what was built in our children's souls by the state, and the state was trying to demolish in their souls what we were trying to build.

One Way Out of Bondage

And there is only one way out of bondage—celebration and sacrifice. Very often in Romania we have realized that they managed to have police for everything—for what we ate, for what we were not supposed to eat. Every time we had a shortage, for instance, of butter, they were discovering in our newspapers that butter induces cancer. Every time we didn't have eggs, they were suddenly discovering that eggs were very, very unhealthy for the human body. Every time we didn't have something, we said, "Here they come, here they come. This is unhealthy again." And we all knew, but everybody had to eat something.

That reminds me of something we joked about. An old gentleman really had a problem with his health one day on the street, and he leaned toward a wall and wanted to catch his breath. While he stayed there, somebody, thinking that they were going to open up a shop or sell something to eat, started lining up behind him. So it was—one, two, three, four and finally the thirtieth, looking at his watch, said, "Excuse me, what are we waiting here for?" The twenty-ninth said, "I don't know." The twenty-eighth is asked, and he doesn't know, and finally the line gets to the first one, who is now feeling better.

"Sir, why are we standing here? What do we wait for?"

"I don't know."

"But you were the first in line."

"Yes, I felt so bad I leaned on the wall to catch my breath, and I have seen the people are starting to line up behind me."

"How do you feel?"

"I feel all right now."

"Then why don't you go home?"

"Why go home, when I'm first in line?"

In this situation we understood that bondage is when you exchange your life for food. We realized finally that we were actually chewing up our lives by allowing them to be exchanged for garlic, for fish and a cucumber just as the Israelites did.[5] Bondage will come if we are not careful.

I would encourage you, whether you agree with all of it or not, to read the new book by Larry Burkett, *The Coming Economic Earthquake*.[6] It is provocative and thought-provoking.

The politicians do not have the ultimate answer for the economy, morality, or ethics. The answer comes by faith. We need to pray for the leaders of our land that the Spirit of God would stir us and them for His glory. We need a stirring. We need revival. We need spiritual awakening. Much of the fight which we fight today will be over when souls are changed by the power of God's Spirit through Jesus Christ.

Notes

1. According to Louis Drummond, Billy Graham Chair of Evangelism and Church Growth in Samford University's Beeson Divinity School, tales from the American Great Awakening and the Welsh Revival of 1904-06 are part of an

oral tradition among ministers. Without questioning their historicity, he said these are almost impossible to document.

2. *Ibid.*

3. John Knox. Inscription on Reformation Monument, Geneva, Switzerland.

4. Quoted by John Bartlett, *Familiar Quotations* (Boston: Little, Brown and Co., 1955), 86.

5. Ovidiu Bulzan, pastor of Golgotha Baptist Church, Arad, Romania, in sermon at First Baptist Church, Wichita Falls, Texas, on February 16, 1992.

6. Larry Burkett, *The Coming Economic Earthquake* (Chicago: Moody Press, 1991).

3

Rebuild the Walls in America Today

By H. Edwin Young

We need a lot of things in Christianity today, but I think first and foremost we need three things: leaders, leaders, leaders. We need leaders who will stand up and be counted, even in tested, difficult times.

Nehemiah was the consummate leader. He had what it took. I believe Nehemiah could sit down today with Peter Drucker and inform this great business guru about being the right kind of leader. I won't belabor the point, but I think we need to put Nehemiah into some sort of historical perspective. In all probability, he had never been to the Holy Land. He had never been to Israel. When he felt the call of God and the commission of God to go, he had never been to Jerusalem. He was born probably in Susa, the capital of Babylon. He was brought up there in a God-fearing Jewish home. He was probably instructed by his father, as was the tradition, to think about Jerusalem, to think about the homeland. Throughout the history of the Jewish people, the thoughts of believing Jews were never far from Jerusalem. His father probably said to him many, many times, "One day we will

23

go back. One day a leader will arise. One day we will return from being scattered over the face of this earth by those who oppress us." Such was the dream of Nehemiah.

I identify with that. My dad said to me many, many times down in the bucolic area of southern Mississippi where I was reared, "Edwin, make a difference. Edwin, make a difference." And he told me his daddy told him the same thing. It was just sort of a tradition in our family. He would say it a million different ways. He said, "When you leave this world, leave it a little better than you found it." Those were his exact words: "Make a difference."

I believe that is what Nehemiah heard. That was the atmosphere of a God-fearing home where the Lord could speak to His people. Notice, then, the procedure that Nehemiah went through as he felt the call of God. Nehemiah 1:1-4 says:

> The words of Nehemiah the son of Hachaliah. And it came to pass in the month Chisleu, in the twentieth year, as I was in Shushan the palace, That Hanani, one of my brethren, came, he and certain men of Judah; and I asked them concerning the Jews that had escaped, which were left of the captivity, and concerning Jerusalem. And they said unto me, The remnant that are left of the captivity there in the province are in great affliction and reproach: the wall of Jerusalem also is broken down, and the gates thereof are burned with fire. And it came to pass, when I heard these words, that I sat down and wept, and mourned certain days, and fasted, and prayed before the God of heaven.

We Must Do What Nehemiah Did

Before we begin to do a work for the Lord in the world, we need to follow this same procedure. If we do not, we may be trying to build a 1-A world with 4-F material. What did Nehemiah do?

First of all, he asked. Before we begin to do a work for God, we need to ask some questions. We need to ask the right people at the right time with the right intensity bottom-line type of questions. We need to ask questions. Nehemiah did. He asked his brother. He asked other friends who perhaps had gone back and tried to rebuild the city under Zerubbabel or Ezra. He got a firsthand report. There were people who knew what was going on in Jerusalem, so he simply asked them.

Not only did he ask, but it says he heard. We ask a lot of questions, but we are ineffective as listeners. I saw a teenage boy who was asked, "Son, when you think of your daddy, what do you see?" He said, "A big mouth." He was asked, "Son, what would you like to see?" And he answered, "A big ear." We not only have to ask the right questions of the right people at the right time, but we have to really hear. We do not need to have some presupposed, preunderstood, or preinterpreted answers. We need to ask openly, and then we need to listen to what is being said.

Nehemiah Listened for God's Voice

Nehemiah didn't make that mistake. He asked and listened. Then he said, "I sat down." He was not like an American. We are activists. We ask, and if we listen, we are ready to move. We are ready to go. After Nehemiah asked, he listened, and then he sat down. He did not get in a hurry. We don't know exactly how long he sat—days went by, but he sat and thought of visions of God. He got a true vision of God first. He had an idea of what he was up against and what was really going on in Jerusalem. I think he could see why Zerubbabel, Ezra, and the wonderful people who had gone back with them with great goals, ideas, and ways to make a difference in that whole area of the country had basically failed.

What did he do when he sat down? He wept. As he saw the true situation in Jerusalem, he mourned. He mourned with passion, brokenness, humility, a contrite spirit, and a broken heart. Then he fasted. I don't think it was a planned fast. True fasting occurs when you are so caught up in doing something for God and praying and are in touch with Him and the Holy Spirit to such an extent that you just simply don't have time to eat.

Then, finally, Nehemiah prayed. The people were depressed. They felt disenfranchised. They were being pressured because the wall of Jerusalem was broken down and the gates were burned. The fallen walls provided no parameters, no security. Somebody had even burned down the gates. Then God told Nehemiah to go and be a leader.

Leadership Different from Leading

At this point, perhaps we had better define *leadership*. Webster defines it as "one who has the office or position of a leader." That doesn't do much for me. When you look up the

25

word *leader*, it says, "one who leads." You have to look up *lead* and it says "out front." So I need a practical, functional, illustrative definition of leadership. I think leadership occurs when someone steps out and one or more individuals follow. By this definition, I think you can be a leader and not have leadership. I think you can be a leader, but if people do not continually follow you over a period of time and buy into your dream and buy into the direction you are going, you don't have leadership.

A person can have an office, a title, a pedigree, degrees, position, or rank, and you can say, "Surely that person is a leader," and they will not be a leader at all. I also don't think institutions, churches, organizations, and corporations select people to lead who have real leadership ability unless that church, corporation, or institution is in desperate straits. If given the option, they will play it conservative nine times out of ten. I don't like Lee Iacocca's language, and I don't like what he stands for, but he is a leader.

Nehemiah was that kind of leader. We had better call forth the best in leadership in the day and age in which we live because the walls are down and the city gates are burned. I don't have to spend a lot of time with statistics. It doesn't take many statistics to stagger us. Some 85,500 children go through the divorce of their parents every year. Every minute one American is strangled, stabbed, or killed. The tragedy is, those of us who are called out by God in a special way to be Christian men and women, so many times, are a part of the problem instead of a part of the solution.

So what did Nehemiah do? He dealt with Artaxerxes, who was the king, the potentate, the number one leader of the Medo-Persian Empire. Years before an edict had gone out that the walls of Jerusalem would not be rebuilt. Those walls had been down for 150 years. It had been 60 years since anybody had tried to put one brick on top of another brick. Nehemiah had a firsthand report from empirical witnesses that the walls were down and the gates were burned.

Nehemiah Went with Boldness

So Nehemiah went to Artaxerxes and said, "I want to be able to go. I feel the call of the God of heaven." Nehemiah must have had the look of authority. Through the praying of Nehemiah, Artaxerxes was moved. He changed. He didn't say, "You can just go." He said, "I'm going to give you a letter, and you're going to be governor of that area. I'm going to send an armed guard along with you. I'm going to give you permission to go through all the different lands and different areas so you will not be bothered as you travel to Jerusalem."

The trip from Susa, the capital of Babylon, to Jerusalem was about 800 miles and took about two and a half months. Nehemiah 2:11 says, "So I came to Jerusalem, and was there three days." He didn't make a big show when he arrived. Logically, we would have shown our credentials. We would have said, "I'm the man in charge here. This is what I propose to do." He had everything he needed to set up camp, but he didn't do anything for three days.

Then Nehemiah said, "I arose in the night, I and some few men with me; neither told I any man what my God had put in my heart to do at Jerusalem" (Neh. 2:12). I love that phrase—"Neither told I any man what my God had put in my heart." So many times in my life when I felt a strong impression from God, and I had gone through the disciplines of prayer, fasting, asking, sitting down, and waiting, I would come out of the chute and say, "Boy, let me tell you what God has told me to do and what's going to happen here."

Nehemiah was also a hands-on leader. He gave attention to details. He was not immersed in details, but he gave attention to details. That difference is very important.

He saw that the bricks were there to rebuild the wall. He already had the bricks. He brought the wood along with him. He had a tremendous strategy.

Nehemiah 2:13-16 says:

> And I went out by night by the gate of the valley even before the dragon well, and to the dung port, and viewed the walls of Jerusalem, which were broken down, and the gates thereof were consumed with fire. Then I went on to the gate of the fountain, and to the king's pool: but there was no place for the beast that was under me to pass. Then went I up in the night by the brook, and viewed the wall, and turned back, and entered by the gate of the valley, and so returned. And the rulers knew not whither I went, or what I did; neither had I as yet told it to the Jews, nor to the priests, nor to the nobles, nor to the rulers, nor to the rest that did the work.

Sense of Timing is Important

His sense of timing was terrific. If we are going to be leaders and make a difference in the affairs of this world, we must understand that timing is important. Many times we miss it. So many times we wait too long, but most of the time our tendency is to move too rapidly.

Read Nehemiah carefully, and perhaps you will discover something you have never seen. He assigned the people to build the portion of the wall that was closest to their business or to their residence. We would be more careful rebuilding the wall if it were to be near us permanently. If the invaders come, we wouldn't want them to break in through the wall near us. Nehemiah's strategy meant the wall would be well built, well constructed, and with great conscientiousness. Was he a leader or what?

Nehemiah's wall was not as expansive as the original wall, but I think it was more effective. It was a better-built wall because Nehemiah's workers built where they had a self-interest. That's how our church ministers. If we can let people get involved where they have seen pain, their passion drives them. Many of the young women in our church who work in our Crisis Pregnancy Center had abortions themselves earlier in life. They were heartbroken because of it, confessed their sin, got right with God, and now have a passion to help other pregnant women like nobody else has.

Support Groups Help Hurting People

In our cancer support groups, our leaders are men and women who have cancer or have been victorious over cancer, which gives them a passion like no one else has. In our church's AIDS support ministry those who have children or friends who have tested HIV positive are motivated to help others. We have about 28 different specific support groups, where people who have dealt with their hurt help others.

Look at Nehemiah's attention to detail in verse 17: "Then said I unto them, Ye see the distress that we are in, how Jerusalem lieth waste, and the gates thereof are burned with fire." These folks were born there, but Nehemiah had just gotten there and had only been there three days. He said, "Do you see the walls down? Do you see the gates are burned? Behold, look." Sometimes someone from the outside can come in and see things that we have lived with too long and have started to accept. Nehemiah came in with a fresh word from God, and the people listened to him.

He said, "Come, let us rebuild the wall of Jerusalem that we may no longer be a reproach." There was passion in what he was doing. There has to be passion in what we do if we're going to make a difference. When you get on the devil's turf, don't be surprised when the bombs start going off and the daggers and knives start coming. Expect it. If you do not have that, you are not doing anything for God.

Then in verse 18, Nehemiah said, "Then I told them of the hand of my God which was good upon me." Then the people said, "Let us rise up and build. So they strengthened their hands for this good work." For 150 years the walls were down, and for 60 years they tried to do something and failed time after time. That is when it is time for God's man to do something.

The world we live in today is very much like those downed walls and burned gates in Nehemiah's day. Our nation's morals lie in ruin, our ethics are all but destroyed. Crime, murder, abuse, homosexuality, and 1,001 other sins are ravaging our land. Like Nehemiah, we want to do something but can't seem to get going.

Our Nehemiah Project Registers Voters

In our church we started something we call the Nehemiah Project. I believe every eligible person should be registered to vote. We have registration tables about three months out of the year at every exit leading from our church. We almost don't let you go to Sunday School unless you're registered to vote! We don't tell anybody how to vote. I never endorse a candidate, but I speak on issues. The form we use asks that the registering person "fill in your name and address" and other important information and "have five friends to do the same, add yourself to the wall of protection for your family." We ask registrants to vote in their party's primary elections, and to attend their party's precinct meeting after the voting is over. On the back of the form is this statement:

> The mission of the Nehemiah Project is to protect family values in our nation. Like the walls of Jerusalem, my country's walls of morality, justice, and compassion have crumbled with us. With God's help, Nehemiah rebuilt the walls of Jerusalem by assigning each family a section of the wall to repair. With our Nehemiah Project we can rebuild our wall by showing up together at our precinct meetings.

Some 690 people signed up in 1992 to be in their precinct meetings. Some ran for precinct chairman. Again, we don't instruct our people what to believe and what to do, nor do we inquire whether they're Democrats or Republicans. When a person attends a church that believes in the infallible Bible and every Sunday School teacher teaches God's Word and the sermon is built on the Bible, nobody has to be instructed about how to vote on any moral issue, because the Word of God and faithful proclamation have already laid the groundwork.

Ministry—social ministry—is rebuilding the walls and putting up doors and gates.

PART II

Defining
Separation of
Church and State

4

Separation of Church, State, and Religious Liberty

By Lynn R. Buzzard

The phrase *separation of church and state* has become for many people the premiere slogan with which all constitutional questions are addressed and disposed. I want to examine the adequacy of that image in terms of both its strengths and liabilities, and particularly in the context of Baptist theological commitments and our Baptist experience.

It is crucial that we understand the context in which the constitutional issues of church and state are fought today. This context is one of enormous moral and spiritual crisis in the country. This crisis is often described as like an earthquake. Professor Allan Bloom has spoken of the closing of the American mind and the abandonment in the university of any quest for ultimate values. He suggests that relativism has extinguished the real purpose of education, which was the search for the good life.[1]

We don't need scholars to tell us about some of these crises because we see them in our homes, our children, and all sorts of statistics. Among the thousands of illustrations I could use are two: (1) The amount of cocaine confiscated in the United States increased more than 600 percent between 1984 and 1989.[2] (2) The federally funded National Endowment for the Arts has used government money to fund the production of pornography that 20 years ago the vast majority of Americans would not have believed possible. Everywhere we look we see evidence of our nation's collapsing values and morality.

Church/State Issues Are Worldwide

Discussions about church and state are no longer merely a domestic issue. This has become a worldwide issue, particularly in the former Soviet Union, where old gods have been abandoned and the entire society is undergoing a serious quest for new ways on which to build society. How can the former Soviets recover some of the values which once shaped their society? A Russian member of parliament observed to me recently that the people in her country are now seeking to recover what America has thrown away. While Russians seek new spiritual values, enormous secularizing forces continue to sweep through societies such as ours. We see attempts by political factions in some countries to co-opt religion.

Amid all of these cultural and worldwide concerns and changes swirling around us, the phrase *the wall of separation* has become a pivotal point of discussion. It is almost an invocation that is given at any conference on church and state. It has become a type of constitutional chant, which, for many people, is supposed to silence all further discussion. That is, whenever a question arises, someone simply raises the flag of "separation of church and state," and we're all supposed to say, "Oh, yeah. We forgot," and discussion is supposed to cease. Many Baptists are fond of this phrase and use it like an invocation. Like Roman Catholics before a sacred symbol, these Baptists genuflect before the wall and wail, lest it be breached in some way.

The phrase *the wall of separation* does not occur in the U.S. Constitution. The Supreme Court has made clear that there is no single constitutional caliper or figure of speech which can resolve many of the complex questions of church and state. Yet, this phrase has become a symbol for a specific set of attitudes and perspectives about church/state relations in this country.

The Slogan Does Have Some Valid Perspectives

Let me hasten to say here that the slogan does, particularly for us Baptists, reflect some valid sentiments and perspectives. These are appropriate and powerful and need to be affirmed by us. The Baptist experience includes a long history in many nations as a dissenter people. We are a people who have experienced oppression at the hands of religious majorities, often other Christian groups. That history invites us to special sensitivity to certain kinds of questions.

One area in which the image is legitimate is that involving the danger of government adopting a particular religion and using that as a tool for excising and squeezing all other religious viewpoints. Any context in which government appropriates the holy for itself—when it becomes the possessor and the guardian of the faith in a kind of divine-right sort of sense—properly invokes a demand for separation of church and state. When government misuses religion, it invites a similar invocation. Whenever the state takes the place of God, we might properly talk about the importance of a wall of separation.

The editors of this book, Dr. Richard D. Land and Louis A. Moore, and I spent a week in December 1991 in the Republic of Georgia. We met with government officials and Orthodox Church officials on behalf of the Baptist community there. We were disturbed when government officials constantly indicated to us that the issues surrounding the Tbilisi Baptist Church's right to press permits or new property would have to be resolved with the permission of the Orthodox patriarch. In a meeting with then Georgian President Eviad Gamsakhurdiya, we noted our surprise and concern over such a policy, to which he replied, "Well, that's the political reality here."

Indeed, this "political reality" is a major concern in the old Soviet empire, particularly throughout rural parts of Russia and many of the former Soviet republics. As the Orthodox Church resurges in that part of the world and attempts to capture special privileges and places for itself, it often seeks to exclude other Christians. Such actions illustrate the potential for a linkage between church and state in an inappropriate way. The notions of separation of church and state appropriately address this problem.

Politicians Are Tempted to Try to Use Religion

A second area in which the image is appropriate occurs where we see the political use of religion. There will always be a temptation on the part of any political faction or political forces to attempt to align themselves with some religious group in order to get their publicity and support. It has occurred in the United States, and I suspect it will occur again. For instance, politicians seeking office often court members of the Evangelical community, promising allegiance. This is a fraud. It is a misuse of religion. It is an attempt by a political faction to temporarily ally itself with a religious group, only to be divorced after the election. In such context, Christians and Baptists appropriately speak of the importance of separation of church and state and the inappropriateness of that kind of political use of religion.

A third area involves the dangers created by the increasingly regulatory state. The problem today of religious liberty in the United States is primarily not a problem of overt oppression. The most serious problems are the realities of expanding and regulatory state and federal governments that squeeze religion out on a piecemeal basis, regulation by regulation, justified by "public policy" and "compelling state interest" until the distinctives of the church and its witness are destroyed. The traditional imagery of fighting this in terms of the Establishment Clause is often not very effective. The regulatory state can be just as destructive to the distinctives of religious faith as can a hostile state. In fact, it can be worse, because the hostile state must be open about it, and it invites prophetic response and perhaps even civil disobedience.

The state which is out to do us "good" is the most dangerous state. It deludes itself about its real, ultimate purposes. This type of state invites us to recognize the importance of the Free Exercise Clause. In one sense, the Free Exercise Clause is now the most critical protection that the church has. Most of the questions in the constitutional arena today are not Establishment Clause cases about how much the government can side with the Christians but really crucial questions about what limits exist against government intrusion, regulation, and management of Christians, their ministries, and their witness. To what extent in an increasingly regulatory society will the Free Exercise Clause provide some protection, particularly for dissenter traditions which emphasize special perspectives and values and want to be different?

Smith Case Created a Crisis

The Supreme Court's decision in *Employment Division v. Smith* created a constitutional crisis. Justice Antonin Scalia,

35

one of the supposed conservatives, wrote an opinion which basically stripped the Free Exercise Clause of what almost every constitutional lawyer in the United States had long assumed was a fundamental and analytical model. That model required the government to establish a compelling state interest whenever it intruded upon a sincerely held religious belief and that the government regulation be the least restrictive means to achieve that interest. Scalia and majority said no such compelling interest is now required. In fact, they said it had never been required, to which most constitutional history professors say "nonsense." The Court's ruling has created a serious threat to its credibility. The Court is now saying whenever the government has a neutral regulation, as long as it is of general purpose and effect, there is no special protection and sensitivity to the fact that it may intrude upon sincerely held religious beliefs. In the context of the regulatory state, that can be a serious infringement in the long run on religious liberty. It means the Court will now not be a protector of religious liberty because the state almost never will set out deliberately to target religion. It will almost always be in the context of a supposedly neutral regulation. So *Smith* poses a devastating effect on the free exercise model.

Before *Smith*, Courts Not Sensitive to Free Exercise Clause

Most observers suggest the change was under way long before *Smith.* Even though the Free Exercise Clause and this compelling state interest requirement were in effect before *Smith*, the courts had been extremely deferential to government in finding compelling interest. In fact, the courts had often found that certain activities were not even religious, so that only activities that occurred within the worship center of the church would count. Following this line of thinking, churches are very free to carry on worship activities—to pray and sing gospel songs—but they are not free to venture beyond the worship boundary. The minute they do something, such as education, then the court can say, "Oh, you're not doing church now. You're doing education, so you don't get your religious protection." As a matter of fact, before *Smith* the courts were not particularly sensitive to free exercise and its distinctives and uniqueness, but rather were under enormous social and legal pressure to make churches conform. That situation should be of particular concern to people with a dissenter tradition, such as Baptists.

The most troubling thing about the *Bob Jones University* decision several years ago was this same issue. The court said Bob Jones University was not entitled to tax exemption because it didn't conform its practices to fit public policy. Public policy thus became the test for tax exemption. Tax exemption became a reward for staying in step with public viewpoints.

I hold no brief at all for the particular policies of Bob Jones University, but the notion that government privileges are to be passed out to religious groups based on whether their viewpoints conform to the government's viewpoints is a most serious policy. This and other illustrations suggest to me that there are areas in which the traditional images of the wall of separation and separation of church and state are appropriate and consistent with our Baptist heritage.

Nevertheless, in other instances *the wall of separation of church and state* does not serve us well. In fact, instances exist where these words produce dangerous distortions. Throughout this discussion, please keep in mind that the phrase itself does not occur in the Constitution. Many of us believe the form of separation of church and state now advocated by many who use that phrase was clearly never intended by the framers of the Constitution. In fact, I believe anyone who suggests that is either ignorant or dishonest. The framers did not intend what we have today. It may or may not be good policy today, but it is clearly not what the framers intended.

Many of Thirteen Colonies Had Established Churches

Mark DeWolf Howe, a former Harvard professor, said, "The Supreme Court has a right to make history but not to rewrite it."[3] History is clear that many of the original 13 states had established churches and many other forms of preference for religion, including particular religions, and that the framers of the Constitution had no intention of creating a modern secular state. There is a tendency of people who use the slogan to try to view the framers through today's filters that project onto them our current definitions rather than the definitions by which they lived.

Because of the way it is used in the context of court decisions, this distorted image of separation invites us to think of these issues of church and state as primarily and principally "legal" questions that ought to be solved by constitutional historians or people who went to law school. In reality, this legal language often masks the underlying philosophical and political questions that are at the core of church/state issues. Chief Justice Burger, Robert Bork, and many others have pointed out that the modern court doesn't do only law. The modern court does policy and philosophy, too. The notion that these questions are resolved textually by constitutional scribes is simply erroneous. These are not mere legal turf wars. These are not mere questions that are in some corner of a constitutional law book in a chapter called "Freedom of Religion." Fundamental to the questions of church and state are basic questions of philosophy, theology, and political thought. They are not resolved by the invocation of the phrase, *the wall of separation* borrowed from Jefferson and inserted in a court opinion. As the theologian John Bennett once said, "Law is far too important to be left to lawyers."[4]

Separation Motif Wrongly Divides Life into Religious and Secular

A further way in which the image of separation of church and state distorts proper policy is by encouraging, by its very language, a "separation" of life into different spheres. It invites us to think that life can be divided into the sacred and the secular. It has been used to separate not simply the institutions of church and state, but to encourage and advocate the separation of religion, society, and the separation of moral viewpoints and culture. Thus, the separation motif becomes a sword which cuts asunder the body politic, rooting out and separating public life from its moral and spiritual roots. Such a separation of life into that kind of rigid compartmentalization is both impossible and undesirable.

Richard John Neuhaus has spoken eloquently of the danger of what he calls "the naked public square," in which society is stripped, under some illusion of the Establishment Clause, of its religious and moral principles, and left naked to try to grapple with its identity and meaning without the strength of religious values.[5] Indeed, when one asks what questions our society faces regarding the allocation of world resources, bioethics, human life, employment, and family issues, this is not a day in which we can afford to remove from the body politic the kind of vigorous discussion of values and moral principles which religious beliefs encourage. Dare we engage in these kinds of debates in the public sphere without the informing vision of religious tradition? I think not.

Indeed, any attempt to suggest you can have a neutral public square is similarly doomed to failure. There is no such thing as a neutral environment. As Alfred North Whitehead suggested, "A philosopher of imposing stature doesn't think in a vacuum. Even his most abstract ideas are, to some extent, conditioned by what is or what is not known in the time when he lives."[6] There is no one who comes to political life without some informing philosophy and vision. The question is: What kind of visions and what kind of philosophy will be permitted to compete in the marketplace of ideas?

On one of my trips in recent years to the Republic of Georgia, I met with the Chief Justice of the Georgian Supreme Court. He took me into the lobby of his office building and showed me a vacant display stand. He pointed to it and said, "Until recently, the bust of Lenin stood there. But now we're trying to figure out what to put in its place." His words were powerful symbolism. You cannot have a society without some philosophy as the baseline. Something is going to be there. There are no empty podiums in terms of values. Some values will exist.

Soviets Erred in Not Recognizing Spiritual Resources

Some other Christian leaders and I had an opportunity to visit with Mikael Gorbachev shortly before he stepped down as the President of the Soviet Union. He said one of the great tragedies that led to the demise of the former Soviet Union was the government's denial of spiritual resources. In another meeting, the head of the KGB said to us, "We are now paying the price for the failure to draw on the spiritual resources of our people." We cannot separate public life from moral and spiritual values. To the extent that images of separation of church and state invite us to do that, they do injustice to society and to biblical and Christian tradition, which rejects any such separation. We are not asked as Christians to separate our lives into competing kinds of spheres, one sacred and one secular.

There are some elements in Baptist history which, in a tragic kind of way, have encouraged this separation. Not, of course, within the best of Baptist tradition—not the best of our history. There have been moments in Baptist history when the individualistic and separatist strand, perhaps fostered by a frontier revivalist history, have encouraged the kind of notion that says, "Well, we'll have a kind of spiritual world. We'll surround ourselves. We'll pull the wagons together, defend the faith, and let the world go its own way." This has been alien to our better traditions, which recognized the Lordship of Christ over all of life, the necessity of Christians being salt and light in the world, Judeo-Christian doctrines of creation, and Christian concepts of calling and vocation. These distortions, nevertheless, have played a part in Baptist history and at times may have fed into this erroneous notion that Baptists ought to tend to the church and let the world go its way. In fact, Baptists have not been alone in this. The Evangelical community in this country generally has been caught at times in this trap.

To some extent, it is almost like a deal was made in early American history in which government came to the church and said, "Church, look. We know you're real important. You have an important part to play, and we want to give you some things."

We said, "Well, what have you got?"

And they said, "Well, we'd like to give you 'church.' You can have 'church.' We won't do any church. You can do church."

"Well, that's good. We'll take that. What else?"

And they said, "We're going to give you gospel songs. We won't write any gospel songs. You can have all the gospel songs."

We said, "Great! We love gospel songs. What else?"

"Prayer. You get prayer."

"Oh, prayer! We love prayer. What else?"

"Oh, from 11:00 to 12:00 on Sunday mornings—except during the football season."

And they said, "Oh, we'll take that. What else?"

"How about everything after you die? You get eschatology."

"Hey, great! We'll take eschatology."

While we are basking in the joy of these gifts, the government said to us, "Of course, you understand that if we give these things to you, you need to stay in your place, and we'll take care of education, science, art, and philosophy. You do your thing, and we'll do our thing."

And too much of the church said, "Wonderful! We like that. We'll do our thing."

We're paying the price today for that kind of abandonment of our nation's public affairs. Only now are we beginning to recover the urgency of some of these issues and reject this sort of schizophrenia which infected us. Perhaps the dominance of a semi-Christian sort of subculture in much of our country, particularly the South, may have even contributed to this schizophrenia. We could maintain a kind of formal, radical separation in our lives between public affairs and church when, in fact, the public affairs were deeply shaped by Christian cultural values. That's no longer true. It is no longer true that we can count on the Boy Scouts and public schools to help us raise our kids. The world has radically changed. This notion of separation of church and state can become a dangerous invitation to the kind of separation of our lives into spheres that has cost us so dearly in this country.

The Establishment Clause itself suggests some of these problems. Most of us have no problem with the general framework of the Establishment Clause as the Supreme Court has described it; that is, the classic *Lemon* test simply said that any act of government is unconstitutional if its purpose is to aid or inhibit religion or if its primary effect is to aid or inhibit religion or if it produces a kind of excessive entanglement between church and state either in the form of doctrine or administration. The problem with the Establishment Clause today, and where the "separation of church and state" image is such a disaster, is when the Establishment Clause is used not to provide a neutral playing surface in which all ideas compete and bar the government from giving special favors to religious ideas, but when it is, in fact, used to excise from the body politic all the religious ideas. When used in this way it is no longer a neutralizing device but a skewing device in which it performs a search-and-destroy mission in the public sphere, looking around for any ideas that might be religious and then holding them impermissible.

Religious Expression Now Suspect in Public Schools

Consider, for example, how that works in the public school. No one would doubt that a public school as part of an exploration of issues of sexuality might invite a representative of Planned Parenthood to talk about his or her views. Everyone would celebrate that, or at least celebrate the theory of it, in terms of open discussion. If anyone suggested we might invite someone from a Christian tradition to talk about a Christian perspective on sexuality, immediately many organizations, including some with strong Baptist links, would raise the separation-of-church-and-state banner and insist this was impermissible

41

intrusion. The effect of this kind of use of the Establishment Clause is, in fact, to create an exclusive arena for the secularists. Any idea which is religious or even linked to religion, such as a moral idea with religious heritage, is now suspect.

A suit filed before the United States Supreme Court, which only failed five to four, argued that the Hyde Amendment, which barred federal funding for abortion, was impermissible. Why? Because behind it in part was an idea that had religious roots. That kind of definition of the Establishment Clause points to the problem in our culture today. Religious ideas are now second-class citizens. Flying under the banner of separation of church and state, this erroneous definition of the separation of church and state almost guarantees an increasing dominance by the secularist perspective and exclusion of religious options and alternatives.

The sad reality of this erroneous perspective is that it is held by many devout Christians, including some Baptists. In the crucial *Widmar v. Vincent* decision involving the right to free speech by Christians on the campus of the University of Missouri, campus organizations, attorneys general, judges and the American Civil Liberties Union all argued that on university campuses, even in traditional places of free speech, religious ideas could not be spoken. The rules on that campus then said all kinds of ideas were entitled to compete in that marketplace, except religion. Fortunately, that perspective ultimately did not prevail. The fact that major organizations that shape church/state law in the United States and judges—federal judges—took that position is illustrative of the kind of environment in which we find ourselves today.

I had a client, a second-grader in Seattle, who at Thanksgiving time was assigned by a teacher to write about reasons to be thankful. This second-grader drew a picture of Jesus and turned it in to the teacher. The teacher rejected the drawing, declaring, in effect, "You can't be thankful for that."

The parents went to the principal, and the principal said, "Oh, that's right. You can't be thankful for that in a public school." The school board backed up the teacher and principal.

One of the largest law firms in the city of Seattle wrote a legal opinion and said, "That's right." Now, I think that's clearly not right. The fact that the whole legal machinery and administrative machinery of the school system rallied around that perspective, which denied students their own free-speech rights because they happened to want to talk about religion, is illustrative of the terrible force of this kind of extreme imagery of the separation of church and state.

What Should Be the Baptist Response?

So, what is the appropriate Baptist response to all of this? First, we need to reexamine our images and models. The day in which we live is different, and the issues are different. We no longer live in an age like that of the founding of our country, when the issue was whether one particular religious Christian group was going to get an edge on everybody else. Nor do we live in the 1940s and 1950s, when the "big issue" was whether Roman Catholics were going to take over America, and all the Baptists were nervous and wanted to make sure no money went to their schools. Those aren't the issues today. Yet the language and imagery that is touted are from those eras. Today's issues of vouchers and day-care funds call for a much more complicated analysis. I'm not sure what those answers are, but I'm sure that waving the separation-of-church-and-state flag does not answer those questions.

Beyond just reexamining the images, let me suggest some other issues that should concern Baptists. One is our need to go beyond law. These are not legal questions alone. In fact, if we think that the fundamental questions behind church/state issues are going to be solved by courts, we're going to be terribly disappointed. It is a serious mistake for us to put too much trust in constitutions, laws, and courts. They have their limits. We know the law cannot save us spiritually. We are not saved by politics either. The law, while an instrument of society's moral principle, cannot stand alone. We cannot expect the law to save us when we have failed in discipling, education, and evangelism. The law alone will not prop us up.

Second, within the context of the Baptist community, we need to develop a serious theological conversation about jurisprudence and the state. Such a conversation must be biblically sound, integrative of different disciplines, and able to cite things other than the *Federal Reporter* in deciding church/state questions. After all, Christians ought to be able to cite some authority other than the federal courts. For us, ultimately, the framers of public life are not Jefferson and Madison—not even Scalia and Rehnquist or Bork and Thomas. The framers of an understanding of the public sphere also include our biblical traditions, our Lord, the apostles, and the New Testament. Too often we have confined our conversation about church/state affairs to the discussion of legal materials. Only by a sound foundation in biblical faith can we avoid what I consider to be the extremes of the Reconstructionists or surrender to the double-life people of a radical separation.

It was said of Jesus that He spoke with authority and not as the scribes (Matt. 7:29). We must learn to do the same. It seems to me we speak to one another with authority not when we cite Brennan or Scalia, but when we have a more fundamental perspective shaped by our biblical tradition. Politics must involve theology, and we need not surrender to those who would ask us to leave our theologies at home when we discuss law.

Third, we need to reject openly and candidly the notion that absolutes and moral values must be held privately but not discussed publicly. Only when we are able to discuss ultimates can we deal with the immediates. C. S. Lewis reminded us of the danger of any society that thinks it can castrate and then bid the geldings to multiply. In fact, that is what he suggested has happened to modern education—that we've stripped it of all that gives it character and moral force and then asked it to be our savior. To talk about absolutes and moral values is not to diminish liberty, but, in fact, to give liberty character and focus.[7]

Fourth, we have to recover our prophetic stance, then we have to refuse to be co-opted. We have to refuse to succumb to the lure of being included with all the other important people. Prophets do not get invited to prayer breakfasts. There is a time and place where we refuse to sell ourselves for seats at the supposed positions of power in order to affirm our distinctives. We need to keep in mind that there is no guarantee of fame or success in our faithful proclamation. We so often measure faithfulness by fame, but in biblical faith the call to integrity comes without a supporting cast of wealth or public recognition.

We Need God's Help in This

In fact, often the opposite occurs. When God called Ezekiel, He promised Ezekiel he would *not* be successful. How would you like to have that as a call to ministry? "Ezekiel, you'll never have the Greater Ezekiel Evangelistic Association. You'll have no tape ministry, no TV. What they will know, Ezekiel, is there has been a prophet in their midst." That's all Ezekiel was supposed to do—tell the truth. We must, in recovering this prophetic tradition, be prepared for God's miracle, God's intervention, but also for dry times, alien times, and lonely times.

Finally, we need to remember in all of this what is at risk. Issues of religious liberty and freedom are not simply questions of a free church. Liberty must always be linked to moral and spiritual values. John Adams said that our country was "designed for a religious and a moral people and for no other."[8] Webster said, "Whatever makes men good Christians makes them good citizens."[9] Alexis de Tocqueville, the French observer of American society, said that liberty, unlike despotism, cannot govern without faith.[10]

The whole question of moral and spiritual values in the role of religion is not just a question of the freedom of the church to do its thing. The question is what kind of culture and what kind of society are we going to have in which to rear our children. The issue is the character of our very culture. We are engaged now in a tragic and doomed experiment in this country by those who suggest that you can have culture when the only value is individual liberty. I do not think you can have culture when that is the only informing vision.

Though he wanted at one point in his life to see religion removed from Europe, George Orwell saw clearly what could happen to a culture when religious values were removed. He initially saw religion as part of the tragedy of Europe. He believed if humans could only be free from religion, they would be fulfilled and whole. Later in life, Orwell, like Malcolm Muggeridge, reflected on that and decided how tragically mistaken he had been. When he talked about what had happened in Europe, he wrote:

> For 200 years we had sawed and sawed and sawed at the branch we were sitting on, and in the end, much more suddenly than anyone had foreseen, our efforts were rewarded and down we came. But, unfortunately, there had been a little mistake. The thing at the bottom was not a bed of roses after all; it was a cesspool full of barbed wire. It appears that the amputation of the soul isn't just a simple surgical job like having your appendix out. The wound tends to grow septic.[11]

In a later short story, he gave this powerful image of what happens to a society that forgets its moral, spiritual, and religious roots. He said:

45

I thought of a rather cruel trick I once played on a wasp. He was sucking jam on my plate, and I cut him in half. He paid no attention—merely went on with his meal while a tiny stream of jam trickled out of his severed esophagus. Only when he tried to fly away did he grasp the dreadful thing that had happened to him. It is the same with modern man. The thing that has been cut away is his soul.[12]

Notes

1. Allan Bloom, *The Closing of the American Mind* (New York: Simon and Schuster, 1987), 34-35.

2. *Annual Statistical Report*, Drug Enforcement Administration, reported in *Statistical Abstract of the United States, 1991* (Washington, D.C.: U.S. Department of Commerce), 184.

3. Mark DeWolf Howe, *The Garden and the Wilderness: Religion & Government in American Constitutional History* (Phoenix, Ariz.: Phoenix Books, 1965).

4. John Bennett, "Scope of Law—Scope of Morality" in *Engage/Social Action*, August 1973.

5. Richard J. Neuhaus, *The Naked Public Square: Religion and Democracy in America* (Grand Rapids: William B. Eerdmans, 1984).

6. Alfred North Whitehead, *Dialogues of Alfred North Whitehead* (Westport, Conn.: Greenwood, 1977).

7. C. S. Lewis, *The Abolition of Man* (New York: Macmillan, 1947), 34.

8. John Adams, *The Works of John Adams*, Vol. IX (1856), 22.

9. Daniel Webster, speech at Plymouth, Mass., Dec. 22, 1820. Quoted by John Bartlett, *Familiar Quotations* (Boston: Little, Brown and Company, 1955), 450.

10. Alexis de Tocqueville, *Democracy in America*, trans. Henry Reeve (London: Saunders and Otley, 1835; New York: Alfred A. Knopf, 1945) 1: 318.

11. George Orwell, cited in "Lessons from the Prophets Orwell and Paul for 1984," Robert L. Toms, Christian Legal Society Quarterly 5 (1984):1

12. *Ibid.*

5

The Uneasy Conscience of Modern Fundamentalism: 45 Years Later

By Carl F.H. Henry

When I first wrote of *The Uneasy Conscience of Modern Fundamentalism* in 1947,[1] the scattered and beleaguered evangelical movement in America was in the forenoon of its reconstruction. Five years earlier the National Association of Evangelicals had been founded. From its beginnings it included reawakening interdenominational churches, a growing Pentecostal movement, and a smaller number of evangelicals who exerted merely a marginal influence in their mainline denominations. Almost all had withdrawn from the broader cultural arena.

The major Protestant denominations were dominated increasingly by the theologically modernist Federal Council of Churches, which almost from its beginnings in 1908 had a social agenda that minimized personal evangelism. This Social Gospel trend was jubilantly inherited by the National Council of Churches, which arose in 1950 as a branch of the World Council of Churches. The National Council listed as its charter constituency 29 denominations with 143,000 congregations numbering 33 million church members.

The SBC Largely Went Its Own Way

By contrast, founding participants of the National Association of Evangelicals (NAE) came from 50 mostly smaller denominations, many of them determinedly independent. The Southern Baptist Convention, the largest Protestant denomination in the United States, largely went its own solitary way, although one of its pastors, R. L. Decker, was at one point elected president of the NAE.

Through its multiplying service commissions, NAE soon claimed a constituency of 10 million, many of them members of conservative churches that were struggling to survive effectively in the larger ecumenical arena. Among these service agencies was National Religious Broadcasters, founded in 1943 to protest an ecumenical blockade of evangelical access to the air waves. The theologically inclusive Federal Council had preempted free public service time and then even opposed the sale to conservatives of network time for evangelical religious programming.

When the National Association of Evangelicals was formed in 1942, ecumenical leaders looked with open disdain at the terms *fundamentalist* and *evangelical,* and gloried instead in being characterized as modernist. Their core assumptions were that contemporary science had discredited Christian supernaturalism, social and political changes can shape an ideal world order quite apart from personal regeneration, and history was evolving upward toward the Kingdom of God.

In this context biblically assertive Christians—ridiculed as fundamentalists—concentrated their energies on the church's traditional evangelistic and missionary task and largely withdrew from public cultural engagement. My book *The Uneasy Conscience of Modern Fundamentalism*[2] aimed to overcome that dichotomy and enlist evangelicals for cultural involvement no less energetically than for their dedication to evangelism.

Now, 45 years later, the evangelical outlook is remarkably different. In the intervening half-century evangelical churches have grown so notably in numbers and influence that they are widely regarded as the Protestant mainline, whereas Protestant ecumenism has been largely sidelined.

The Movement Continued to Grow

From the 1947 tent meetings in Los Angeles, the Billy Graham evangelistic crusades expanded into a world ministry in which over 2 million persons are said to have responded to an invitation to accept Christ. Many Christian college enrollments have soared, and evangelicals have launched new and rapidly growing seminaries. The Evangelical Foreign Missions Association (now the Fellowship of Missionary Agencies), formed by 14 charter agencies in 1945, had by 1986 grown to represent 12,464 missionaries serving in more than 130 countries. Established in 1949, the Evangelical Theological Society, affirming the Bible's inerrant inspiration in the original writings, has provided a constructive framework for theological reflection by more than 2,000 scholars committed to the truthfulness of Scripture. Parachurch youth ministries like InterVarsity Christian Fellowship, Youth for Christ, Young Life, Campus Crusade for Christ, and Navigators enlisted tens of thousands of students for evangelical training and service, despite the naturalistic stance of public education. Evangelical publishing houses like Eerdmans and Zondervan thrived; new magazines appeared, paced by *Christianity Today*; evangelical authors provided both scholarly and popular religious literature, including new Bible translations; and evangelical writers with access to large audiences made the best-seller lists. National Religious Broadcasters reported in 1988 that almost 1,400 of the 9,000 radio stations in the United States are religious in nature and that of the 259 religious television stations, most are evangelical in emphasis.

Although often shut out of the corridors of denominational power, many conservative Protestants in ecumenically affiliated communions are now no less interested in social ethics than in personal ethics. They do not, however, focus exclusively on the social mission of the church, nor are they prone to view pragmatic political proposals as inherently Christian. First and foremost, evangelical social emphasis falls on scripturally revealed principles, in contrast to the neoorthodox disavowal of propositional revelation and its emphasis instead on private response to an inner divine command.

Evangelicals led the way, for example, in the worldwide child care and relief ministry of World Vision, founded in 1950 by Bob Pierce, and global outreach to prisoners by Prison Fellowship Ministries, founded in 1976 by Charles Colson. Such major social ministries, curiously, had been neglected by Social Gospel enthusiasts who concentrated mainly on a political agenda.

Evangelicals Were Lifeline of Moral Majority

Evangelicals were the lifeline of the Moral Majority, founded in 1979 by Jerry Falwell as the new Religious Right's political action group. It set Judeo-Christian values over against secular humanism, mobilized support for morally concerned political candidates, assailed vices like pornography and homosexuality, and opposed federally funded abortions and the banning of prayer in public schools. Today evangelicals are nationally active in family ministries like Focus on the Family, led by James Dobson; the pro-life movement of which Operation Rescue is but one statement; and The Christian Legal Society, which champions free religious expression in public schools that prejudicially disallow evangelical Bible study groups while permitting rival gatherings. Evangelicals participate in dialogues sponsored by the Ethics and Public Policy Center, The Institute on Religion and Democracy, and other such efforts. They champion a responsible view of private property and capitalism and promote human rights, especially religious liberty, over against restrictive totalitarian regimes. To be sure, evangelicals were not frontal participants in the marches against American race discrimination. Although biblical principles underlay Martin Luther King's nonviolent protests, many evangelicals feared that massive demonstrations would further jeopardize law and order, and they felt that the courts could best decide the issue.

Agenda Includes Political Participation

The evangelical movement has therefore passed far beyond its initial stages of an uneasy conscience to a stance of political participation and aggressive confrontation and lobbying.

Despite this evangelical effort, the influences that decisively shape contemporary American society are today depicted much more accurately as naturalistic or humanistic, than as theistic and evangelical. This is the case whether one has in view public high schools and state universities, the mass media and literature and the arts, or the national political arena. After allowance is made for the private perspective and policy commitments of a discriminating minority, the fact remains that the cultural high tide today is more pragmatic than principled. It accords little public significance to fixed truth, unrevisable values, or to the will and purpose of God in national affairs. Neither the public schools, nor the media, nor the political arena are today comfortable with the Declaration of Independence's bold affirmation that a supernatural Creator has endowed all humankind with unalienable rights and the consequent grounding of the moral responsibility of the human race in the doctrine of divine creation.

Yet to confront society with a counter-agenda that begins only with horizontal political, economic, ecological, or gender values is to lose the battle for absolutes even before the debate gets under way. If evangelicals taper social action to these limits, the world has little to fear or to learn from evangelical penetration. Even the vision of a "Christian America" loses force if one sacrifices the living God and His articulately revealed will as governing realities. Even the emphasis that the United States faces a diversity and multiplicity of crises—a debt crisis, an education crisis, a savings-and-loan crisis, a Medicaid crisis, a drug crisis, a crime crisis, and so on—focuses merely on symptoms, while it obscures the prime cause and terminal disease of our society, its eclipse of God the Creator and Judge of all humankind.

Diversity, Division Are Obstacles to Evangelicals

The lack of evangelical cultural penetration in depth is not due primarily to evangelical diversity and internal disagreement over public issues. To be sure, diversity exists, and the evangelical impact could be somewhat stronger were its voice unanimous and all evangelicals participated in the political process as actively as they do in evangelistic effort. Yet American evangelicals have themselves uncritically accommodated the obscuring of their own badge of identity. Once disdained by modernists and even by some early neoorthodox spokespersons, the term *evangelical* gained increasing favor as liberalism lost theological precision and signified mainly a political outlook. Even some neoorthodox writers, including Karl Barth, managed to rediscover it, at least in part. Activists who combined theological conservatism with political liberalism were not a decisive force, their commitments being often pragmatic and vacillating. Craig M. Gay's recent book, *With Liberty and Justice for Whom,*[3] which surveys American evangelical perspectives on capitalism, leaves little doubt that evangelical writers were mainly aligned neither on the uncritical right nor on the socialist-tilting left. Some professed to champion the cause of the poor while they spoke only critically of capitalism, only to be embarrassed when the Eastern

51

European masses reached gratefully for a free market and private property and repudiated the socialist experiment as a failure. The evangelical mainstream defends a free market and private property in the context of biblical principles, including divine stewardship and the propriety of legitimate profit.

Aware of the evangelical movement's strength, mediating scholars now routinely emphasize the diversity of evangelicalism as the first stage of an effort to establish their own deviance from it as normative. The champions of deviance frequently elevate their main grievance into a creedal article dwarfing all others.

The real reason evangelicalism has still not deeply penetrated the reigning culture is that the culture—whether on its right or on its left—has too much penetrated the evangelical movement. The *avant garde* improprieties have become the hallmark, if not of ourselves, then of our neglected children and grandchildren. Life for us, as for them, is incomplete without a new car, TV, VCR, or word processor. Pity Jesus, Paul, Isaiah, and Moses that they were deprived of soul-enriching video treasures like the "Golden Girls," "Married With Children," or "Current Affair." Most nauseating of all is "Studs," which even monkeys and chimpanzees would find repulsive.

Spiritual Predicament of America's Christians

The spiritual predicament of many merely professing Christians in America is reflected by a recent Gallup poll. On the one hand it indicates not only that most of the population believes that God exists, but even that Jesus of Nazareth is His Son and the divine Savior. On the other hand, the survey indicates that only six percent to ten percent are "deeply committed Christians" holding a "high spiritual faith," given to prayer, practical life application of their beliefs, and charitable giving. This minority, Gallup notes, truly shares the joy of religious experience. Despite its express rejection of hedonism, it is internally "far happier" than the rest of the population, and externally exerts on communities a disproportionately powerful influence. One is therefore driven to conclude that not only do the great majority of professing Christians count for little in contemporary society, but that internally they are spiritually parched. For many, interest in the transcendent world seems little more definite than a Washington television weatherman's comment during a dry spell: "Keep your fingers crossed, and maybe we'll get some help from above."

Still other recent opinion polls attest to the cultural outlook's diluting impact on Christian doctrine and practice. The Barna Research Group in *What Americans Believe*[4] reports a notable erosion of biblical beliefs. An emphasis on humanity's inherent goodness, self-sufficiency, and complete control of one's final destiny counters any acknowledged need of divine forgiveness, redemption, and spiritual enablement. Almost two in three of the Americans polled postulate that Christians, Jews, Muslims, and Buddhists merely invoke the same God under different names. A generic deity replaces the self-revealing God of the Bible; assurance declines that the deity is a personal being; and New Age and similar movements are welcomed for their promise of "religious renewal." These developments prosper at the expense of an explicitly Christian view of God. Neglect of church attendance, Bible reading, and prayer are components of this trend.

Relativism Is Etching Deep Scars

If it is all the same whether one prays only to a universal force or a supernatural person, and if an impersonal religious process is universally efficacious irrespective of the reality or unreality of the supernatural, and irrespective of divergent spiritual beliefs, then one no longer can assuredly claim a personal relationship to the triune God of Christianity or claim to be on speaking terms with the Judge of the universe. The Barna Report indicates almost incredibly—with a margin of error of 4 percent—a sharp expansion of those now skeptical of any absolute truth, to 62 percent of the people. It further indicates that the figure rises to 74 percent for 18- to 25-year-olds, or almost three in four, who consider absolute truth an illusion. Philosophical relativism, not effectively challenged in the schoolroom, is etching deep scars on society at large and unsettling the churches as well.

The Barna Report indicates also that almost two out of three American adults (63 percent) consider the purpose of human life to be "enjoyment and personal fulfillment."[5] Society is increasingly impelled by the maxim "If it feels good, do it." Almost six in ten (56 percent) consider the emphasis "God helps those who help themselves" to be biblically based.[6]

Present-day Americans volunteer less time to worthy causes and organizations than in the recent past. Born-again

Christians are less likely to reduce volunteer time than are non-Christians. Yet the Barna Report indicates that evangelicals and Roman Catholics are now less inclined to volunteer time for church-related activities than are adults in mainline Protestant churches.[7]

The Barna Report reminds us that, while 35 percent of the adult population in the United States affirms a personal commitment to Jesus Christ as Savior and says that it is born again, this leaves unreached two out of three American adults.[8] More than half of those attending church next Sunday (about 52 percent) "will not be born again Christians."

Unchurched Still Seek Relationship to God

Half the unchurched (49 percent) consider a close relationship with God to be desirable, and almost half of all adults (47 percent) think the Christian faith is "relevant to the way they live." Yet only 28 percent regard their nearby local church as similarly relevant.[9] The secular caricature of church doctrine has taken an erosive toll. Whereas Jesus depicted His redemptive ministry as the overthrow of Satan and his minions, 60 percent of Americans now consider Satan merely a literary symbol of evil.

Except for the elderly, most adults presently spend somewhat less time than a year ago watching television, largely due to a deterioration of programming. Some 30 percent of adults also spend less time with friends than in the past.[10] Yet television becomes for most not only our national entertainment but our nourishment. The "prince of the power of the air" packages the appeal to lust in the sultry voice of temptation with visual art and color graphics. One can hardly zap the prime-time channels, even on public television, without finding a sex-hungry male and female frolicking in bed; some leering sexpot enticing consumers to buy soft drinks, beer, perfumes, or automobiles; or without hearing Christ's name taken in vain.

A couple of decades ago one could still find among television executives devout church-going leaders with at least some ethical regard for network programming as a public trust, whereas today the commercial instinct reigns supreme. If stripteasing yields the highest audience ratings, it gets the nod. In the name of sexual liberation, the inherited virtues are cast to the winds; self-discipline and the postponement of gratification belong to another era. Ratings-hungry programs feature all variety of deviance, declaring it not sensational or controversial but rather a window on modern life. Even network news programs, which do manage to preserve a minimally informative role, cope constantly with an entertainment impulse. Faced by shrinking audiences and sagging profits, the networks may soon face the day when the presence or absence of a G-string may decide their destiny. For multiplied dollars they discard modesty, decency, and chastity. Sexual liaison, near-nudity, and vulgarity now are the hallmarks of more and more television films. Popular magazines today report pregnancies and births to unmarried movie stars as if marriage were now an unnecessary encumbrance.

In the Oxford University Press publication *The Rise of Selfishness in America*[11] the social historian J. L. Collier warns that self-indulgence has carried the United States to the brink of doom and only a rebirth of selflessness can now spare it. Americans ridiculed earlier Victorian repression only to replace it by something worse, the forfeiture of a sense of moral duty. Multitudes now consider self-gratification ideal in matters of love, sex, child-rearing, politics, and even religion.

Evils Fill American Bedrooms

Millions of American bedrooms and living rooms, Collier says, now accommodate evils once confined to red-light districts and segregated vice sections of the big cities. Today 40 percent of American children are "conceived before the woman's first marriage."[12] "Monogamy is gone, both as an ideal and a practice," he says.[13] Only 7 percent of American households are now comprised of a working father, stay-at-home mother, and dependent children. We have accommodated "the disappearance of the traditional family."

According to Sharon Grinage, founder of the newsletter *Divorced and Widowed Women's Network*, more than 50 percent of U.S. marriages end in divorce. Some 18 million children, or 61 percent of those under age 18, live with single mothers, and nonsupport is a major cause of poverty among children.

America's shirking of parental responsibility is "unmatched in human history," Collier comments.[14] Many parents now accept no responsibility for the children they propagate. Divorce rates have doubled since 1965. Despite the belief widely held that a single parent can equally well raise a child, "in no known human society, past or present," says Collier, "have children been generally raised outside of an intact

55

nuclear family."[15] Given present trends, most American children are likely by century's end to spend most of their childhood in day-care centers.

Although Victorians violated their own ideals, Collier comments, they at least "set for themselves goals of social concern, charity, self-control, a decent regard for the welfare of others, a willingness to protect the weak."[16] In their place a new ethic has arisen whose first loyalty is not to family but to "the self."[17] The new ethic replaced the Christian view that human nature has inherited an Adamic passion that needs to be restrained. It substituted the emphasis that the free expression of basic feelings will make humans happier. This notion, that human nature is a malleable blank slate, writes Collier, is "perhaps the most important . . . change of mind in modern times."[18]

The behavioral revolution in America, Collier insists, took place in the 1970s—not in the Great Depression, or during or after World War II, or in the 1950s or 1960s. "What had been a rare, even scandalous life-style in 1960 was by the 1970s commonplace."[19] The permissive sexual trend was spreading from collegians to noncollegians and to high school students. By 1973, 28 percent of boys and 10 percent of girls had intercourse by age 13 or younger. In society at large "permissiveness with affection" was yielding to "recreational sex." High school and young adult involvement with drugs soon exceeded that of any other industrialized nation on earth. By 1970 addicts numbered between 100,000 and 200,000, not including between 12 and 20 million Americans who had used marijuana at least once.

The phenomenon that quickly came to characterize the new America, Collier emphasizes, was television. It soon dominated leisure time, isolated the self from fellow humans, and turned viewers into mute spectators. "Nothing, perhaps, since the discovery of alcohol," writes Collier, "has so dramatically altered the nature of human consciousness as television," which for many Americans is now "the central element in their lives."[20] In 1972-73, when the behavioral revolution was surging ahead, Americans bought 34 million television sets, even though 97 percent of the homes already had a set. Television plunged viewers into a fantasy world, accelerated violence, and duped children through commercials; erotica that the Victorians curtailed now became easily accessible. "The overwhelming majority" of Americans spend more time in front of a television set, says Collier, "than they do at anything but work or sleep."[21] Between 10 percent and 33 percent of viewers are literally addicted to it.

Decline in Sexual Morality Is Obvious

The number of marriages per 1,000 population declined in 1988 to the lowest level since 1967. Sociologists more concerned with statistics than with morality think the difference is largely offset by unmarried people living together, and some explain it by increased education, as if ignorance and the traditional morality go hand in hand. One-third of American women ages 25 to 29 indicated in 1988 that they had at some point cohabited outside of marriage. Morton Kondracke, of *The New Republic*, notes that before age 18 more than half of American white women and about three-fourths of black women are now sexually active, that two out of three black babies are born out of wedlock, and that 40 percent grow up on welfare. To the immorality of abortion—1,600,000 fetuses destroyed annually—we must now add the fact that a child is abused somewhere in this nation every two seconds.

Although the Centers for Disease Control place at 187,000 the number of those in the United States who are known to have contracted AIDS, the actual number infected with the virus—mostly through sexual contact or sharing of needles by drug users—is widely estimated at a million persons. One actress has recently remarked that 50 percent of her friends have died of AIDS. Many in the gay community are prone to argue that homosexuality is a matter of brain structure rather than of morality. The permissive media tend to view as a matter of prejudice any criticism of victims of AIDS, even when contracted by fornication. A *Washington Post* headline announced that Magic Johnson's affliction by it could "help end the stigma of AIDS." In 1990 the United States spent $1.5 million on AIDS, which has claimed 126,000 lives in a decade. This is as much as it has spent on cancer, which in a single year kills four times as many persons.

To be sure, the answer to the sex crisis is not universal celibacy—which would deprive humankind of a posterity except by fornicating parents. Nor is it sexual profligacy, which undermines social stability, marital virtue, and interpersonal integrity. The gratuitous distribution of condoms to high school students merely encourages sexual experimentation; it guarantees neither safe nor moral sex. Castration or vasectomy for serial rapists might send a better signal than a brief prison interlude.

God Designed Responsible Intercourse

The Creator of life entrusted humans with responsible intercourse within monogamous marriage, both for procreation and pleasure. The cure for this generation is a dose of regenerative religion and biblical morality, a new generation that focuses on the greatness of God and primacy of His will.

In reentering the public arena, some few persons on the evangelical left elevated the priority of changing social structures above that of personal evangelism. The wide erosion of personal morality and spirituality in American society evidences that sound legislation and political structures, important though they are, do not of themselves assure a model society. Not alone the evangelical left has underestimated the importance of evangelism; however, many evangelical churches have dwarfed the evangelistic mandate except by way of verbal commendation. Only a minority of members are involved in personal evangelism other than by financial support for crusades and movements.

Christians Must Face Their Culture

Televangelists such as James Bakker, Oral Roberts, Jimmy Swaggart, and Robert Tilton meanwhile have revived the public misperception of evangelical evangelism in terms of Elmer Gantry manipulation and exploitation. These efforts connect evangelism with the assurance of miraculous healing more than with a revival of prayer. Evangelicals desperately need a return to prayer meetings burdened for national righteousness and spiritual renewal of the churches as well as for the salvation of the lost. To pray for rulers—not only to displace them—is part of our political duty.

Public responsibility includes participation in the political process, and not alone by critical confrontation. Although evangelicals have reentered the culture, many maintain no significant tie to their elected representatives, even as they cultivate few neighborly relationships with unchanged townspeople. The cult of self-expression and self-gratification has taken deep root within the evangelical community itself. Dr. James D. Hunter, a University of Virginia sociologist, has noted that the traditional stress on self-denial in evangelical theology and preaching has given way to an emphasis on self-fulfillment, and that some popular pulpiteers have built large congregations by proclaiming the basic legitimacy of the self's aspirations. The so-called "health and wealth philosophy" affirms that only a lack of faith frustrates complete fulfillment of the self's desires. Whoever approves these notions, which the special economic privileges of modern Western society readily accommodate, should not be surprised that, in direct contradiction of Judeo-Christian doctrine, New Age and other modern pantheistic cults readily invade such circles to portray the self additionally as an aspect of divinity.

To confront the national addiction to self-indulgence is no easy task for an evangelicalism itself deeply invaded by a materialistic entertainment culture. Only to a somewhat lesser degree than the secular culture are many evangelicals today victimized by the spirit of the age. To an unregenerate society it seems regressive to question the moral worth of the modern media, of avant garde fashions, of pornography, or of indulgence in drugs, alcohol, and sexual infidelity. All these things are viewed as having a legitimate and desirable place in the life of the quintessent modern self. That fact does not of itself, however, establish propriety or morality. What it attests, rather, is that contemporary man is losing interest in the question of whether activities are moral or wicked, and wants only to know—as did ancient Sodom and Gomorrah—whether they are pleasurable.

Evangelical religion remains one of humanity's last defenses against "the cult of the self." It offers a regeneration of the self that can supply the moral and spiritual power requisite to resist, challenge, and rectify the domineering pagan mind that now seeks to monopolize all of modern life.

What our civilizational dilemma obscures is a proper appraisal of human character. Nonbiblical views seek the ideal self by realigning or rebalancing fallen humanity's present nature. Christianity holds that the ideal self is attainable only through the spiritual crucifixion of the unregenerate self and the birth of a new self through the transforming work of the Spirit of God with its distinctive constellation of values. The biblical analysis of human nature—of man bearing God's image, flawed now by ethical rebellion, and yet by divine grace offered spiritual regeneration and a role in the moral recovery of a culture sinking out of control—can lift a deviant society again to the level of genuine blessing and durable hope.

The effort to rebalance an unregenerate selfhood soon deteriorates into hedonism despite fallen humanity's best effort due to an exemption of possessions and sexual behavior from moral accountability.

The Urgent Task for Christians

The urgent task that now falls largely to the people of God is to champion the moral cause of the nuclear family, of social decency, of institutional justice, and of cultural concord, and to claim once again for Christ and His Kingdom the now renegade realms of literature and the arts, including music. We need to counter sweeping current proposals to organize society around the motif of hedonistic pleasure, the unbridled satisfaction of consumer lusts, and the degrading entertainment industry.

We do this best by a powerful reminder, in word and deed, of spiritual and moral ultimates that make human existence worthwhile and meaningful. To call the nation to put God first, to strive for societal decency, to display a model of personal godliness and public justice, to return to the house of prayer for spiritual renewal, to reach a confused citizenry with the good news of God's grace, to exude the joy of God in a climate of shameful violence, and to promote truth in the nation's executive offices, justice among judges, integrity among legislators, dignity in the media, impartiality by journalists, industry among workers, and equity by management—every such gain we register, alongside a recognition of our own limits and needs, is a service that looks toward the Kingdom of God.

Unless Christians now swiftly comprise a moral counterculture exhibiting a patently different lifestyle, they are only postponing their social irrelevance. If the communes of the sixties involving perhaps no more than 10,000 persons, and then a half million hippies who comprised less than 5 percent of their age group, could impose upon American society a highly distinctive mark, surely 50 million evangelicals—or 30 million if you wish, or even 10,000 dedicated believers, if God can find them—should be able somehow to shake this declining culture to its very roots. Surely 50 million evangelicals will not be held guiltless if they allow the impression to widen that God is indifferent to or is pleased with what is now happening in and to American society.

Morals Are in State of Decline

James J. Kilpatrick comments on the drift of the times: "Everything is sliding downhill. Captains of industry cheat on government contracts. Bankers knowingly violate security laws. Politicians accept 'contributions' that are just short of bribes. In the midst of moral collapse, our society responds, literally and metaphorically, by passing out condoms."[22]

Even leaders who have promoted structural changes in society more than personal morality are beginning to speak out about the nation's ethical and spiritual decline. Benjamin Hooks, former executive director of the NAACP, the nation's oldest and largest civil rights organization, told the *Washington Times*:[23] "The whole philosophy of our country has changed...(to accept) immorality, degeneracy, pornographic movies.... I'm the world's greatest advocate of the First Amendment...but somehow we've got to have freedom with some responsibility." The entertainment media, Hooks said, portray sex and violence in a way that leads to a casual view of murder, lawlessness and teenage pregnancy. "This is a violent society" and the solution may well lie, he added in a recovery of family values, of "Southern Baptist morality," especially the conventional nuclear family with gainfully employed parents.[24]

Hooks does not stand alone in lamenting the nation's serious moral decline. The prominent columnist George Will, writing in *Newsweek*, has depicted the present situation as "America's Slide into the Sewer." Codes of ethics are breached today in business, in government, in interpersonal relations, in the professions, and in religious circles.

The grip of naturalism on American culture is now so pervasive that evangelicals may well be unable by themselves to remedy the social condition. Churchgoers who hope to turn the tide must first pray earnestly for spiritual revival in their own churches; that is, for an outpouring of God's Spirit that purifies our priorities and restores the full joy of the gospel and reinforces its imperatives.

The way to shape an evangelical counterculture is not simply to march on Washington, to get involved in the political process at the precinct level, to descend en masse on congressional offices, to engage in public confrontation that the media delight to cover, to launch boycotts. All such efforts have their indispensable place and time, but they do not nurture a deeply rooted counterculture. It must rise instead in the churches, in the prayer meetings, in members turning out by the hundreds and thousands and tens of thousands seeking renewal, in so many cars suddenly parked near a local church that the world once again becomes curious about what is taking place in those forsaken sanctuaries, and gives new credence to the rumor that God is alive in the history of our times. It must root in changed lives, in members whose new birth 40 years ago is no longer the only referent wherein God became alive for them, in a neighborly interest in townspeople that makes others think that the crucified and risen Jesus may indeed still have hands and feet today. Let the restoration of the prayer meeting be the mirror of a rising evangelical counterculture, one that begins not with the self but with God, and places others, if not before one's self, at least on a par with ourselves, and seeks our shared good in the nation so remarkably blessed by God.

Notes

1. Carl F.H. Henry, *The Uneasy Conscience of Modern Fundamentalism* (Grand Rapids: Eerdmans, 1947).

2. *Ibid.*

3. Craig M. Gay, *With Liberty and Justice for Whom* (Grand Rapids: Eerdmans, 1991).

4. Barna Research Group, *What Americans Believe* (Ventura, Calif.: Regal Books, 1991).

5. *Ibid.*, 300.

6. *Ibid.*, 301.

7. *Ibid.*, 65.

8. *Ibid.*, 297.

9. *Ibid.*, 299.

10. *Ibid.*, 71, 74.

11. J. L. Collier, *The Rise of Selfishness in America* (New York: Oxford University Press, 1991).

12. *Ibid.*, 236.

13. *Ibid.*, 236.

14. *Ibid.*, 252.

15. *Ibid.*, 246.

16. *Ibid.*, 18.

17. *Ibid.*, 48.

18. *Ibid.*, 108.

19. *Ibid.*, 226.

20. *Ibid.*, 168.

21. *Ibid.*, 239f.

22. James J. Kilpatrick, "Praise for a Prude," *The Washington Post*, Aug. 27, 1991, p. A23.

23. *The Washington Times*, interview by Ronald A. Taylor, Aug. 30, 1991:A1.

24. *The Washington Times*, interview by Ronald A. Taylor, Aug. 30, 1991:A1.

PART III

Issues Looming
on the Horizon

6

Religious Liberty as a Cause Celebre

By Carl F.H. Henry

In less than ten years a new century—the twenty-first—
will overtake us. By that time, I predict that religious liberty
may well emerge as the cause celebre of our era.

Such discussion of religious liberty could focus on several
facets, among them that of behavioral determinism, for example, or theological propriety, or civic freedom. The issue of
human liberty reaches far broader and deeper than exploration
only of one's prerogatives as a citizen. Any culture founded
merely on political rights of the individual (such as freedom of
worship and speech) is bound to be less comprehensive than a
culture founded also on duties toward God.

In this present discussion, however, our particular concern is not whether human beings are mechanically or chemi-
cally determined; we are assuming that human beings are
gifted with responsible choice in respect to religion. Neither will
we discuss whether, from a theological or revelational point of
view, humans have a God-given right personally to reject the
living God without penalty. Our emphasis, rather, will analyze

and emphasize religious freedom as a universal civic right. We contend that all human beings, whatever their beliefs, should be protected by their governments from religious repression, recrimination, oppression, and persecution.

Coerced Faith Has No Value

To coerce spiritual belief has no value either to God or humans who are forced to comply against their will. Perpetrators of such religious compulsion invite critical judgment.

The most basic of all human liberties is religious liberty. The choice one makes between the rival gods bears significantly on the definition of justice and human duties and rights.

Pure religion insists that God is to be worshiped "in spirit and in truth" (John 4:24). Nothing attests to the perversity of tyrannical governments more than the fact that two millennia after Christ tyrannical governments still widely thwart the religious freedom of multitudes of human beings.

In the *World Christian Encyclopedia*[1] David B. Barrett reported that in 1980, before the collapse of Eastern European communism, some 2.2 billion people in 79 countries (50.6 percent of the global population) lived under restrictions on religious liberty. They did so, moreover, despite governmental guarantees of religious freedom and written constitutional commitments to the United Nations's *Universal Declaration of Human Rights*. Every world religion has made a sad contribution to such religious oppression; neither Christians nor Muslims nor Jews nor Hindus have been exempt from involvement.

Anyone who thinks that theism should therefore be sacrificed to atheism is a poor student of history and theology. For atheism most of all has spawned the violent oppression and persecution of believers. The Nazi era in Germany, the Communist era in Eastern Europe, and the so-called cultural revolution in mainland China all attest to this. Barrett indicates that the "worst recent case of persecution has been the 1966-67 Great Proletarian Revolution in China. This was history's most systematic attempt ever, by a single nation, to eradicate and destroy Christianity and all religion."[2]

The modern secular state distorts the Protestant Reformation's emphasis on freedom to worship and serve God in accord with a good conscience, into the right of unqualified freedom from God and from religion. Yet religious liberty as a formal civic right embraces even the freedom to espouse atheism. If religious freedom is a fundamental right, it belongs to all.

Although the collapse of Marxism in the Soviet sphere is widely viewed as exhibiting the futility of atheism, atheism retains official political status in mainland China, North Korea, and elsewhere. It remains the metaphysical presupposition of Western secular humanism, which currently shapes the world view of Western university learning. The fundamental philosophical issue facing modernity is whether humans and the universe owe their being and continuance to a supernatural deity or whether all deity-conceptions are of the nature of myth and provide merely a noncognitive way of relating one's self to a nebulous reality beyond historical factuality and conceptual formulation.

Atheism Is Now a Pseudo-Religion

Atheism now often takes the form of a pseudo-religion. Secular humanism manipulates the term *religion* to its own advantage. It holds that religion is conceptually false whenever it designates an objectively existing divinity, while it claims at times to be itself a religion—a religion without a metaphysically existing supernatural divinity. It contends that religion is "true"—that is, productive—insofar as it functions psychologically to deliver its devotees from personality discord, and serves to integrate the otherwise beleaguered self and provide a psychic framework for a more fruitful life. Religion is, in short, psychologically serviceable but is not to be regarded as theologically true.

All the more disconcerting it is that, although Christianity, Judaism, and Islam are theistic religions, they are irreducibly at odds. If Jews a generation ago disproportionately faced the severest persecution during the era of the Nazi holocaust, Christians are at present the main objects of discrimination and persecution. This is, in part, due to the global missionary presence of Christianity. Hostility is invited also by the blow to Islamic pride posed by the technologically superior West, which Islam views as formally Christian, and by contrast with which social critics frequently regard Islamic society as retrograde and degraded. Islam has yet to pass through the scientific revolution.

Muslims Still Persecute Christians

Yet Islamic scholars meanwhile also view the so-called Christian West as retrogressive, and they tend to find compatible links only with liberal theologians who reject the deity of Christ and hence reject also the triune God. The insistence on a unitarian Allah, and on Muhammad rather than Jesus as his supreme prophet, underlies the Muslim creedal antipathy for Christians. The Islamic-Christian clash is the major flash point of religious liberty controversy today. In *A Fragrance of Oppression: The Church and Its Persecutors* Herbert Schlossberg comments that insofar as oppression of Christians is today in view, "if Muslims would cease persecuting the followers of Christ . . . perhaps 90 percent of the problem" would be solved.[3] The main religious sources of the persecution of Christians, he adds, have been Islamic. The fury of Moslem religious hostility to Christianity is approached only by ancient and ongoing hostility between the now largely Islamic sons of Hagar and the Hebrew sons of Sarah. In the Middle East personal identity is ultimately established by one's religious loyalties, whereas in the secular West it is more likely to be established by one's bank balance or one's political preference.

In view of the lifting of restrictions on Christianity by Soviet sphere nations, the repressive treatment of Christian minorities by Islamic nations and Communist mainland China becomes glaringly conspicuous. The situation in Turkey and Egypt is far from desirable, but that in Saudi Arabia is more deplorable.

Saudi Arabia not only refuses to approve of basic religious liberties, but it also withholds from Christians even the *dhimma*, or protection, of the ongoing practice of Christianity.

Saudis Persecute Christians Repeatedly

In line with this outright prohibition of religious activities by non-Muslims, Saudi Islamic police in August 1991 arrested members of a house church. They deported the participants. They then arrested more than 70 Filipino workers attending a *private* prayer meeting in Riyadh. In this same town in October 1991 armed police raided the morning service of a Korean church that was located obscurely on private property. The police detained the entire congregation of 130 adults and 50 children for four hours and confiscated not only all the office equipment, but also all Bibles. When such services are closed down, their leaders lose their jobs and must pay their own airfare home. The Korean government protested the Saudi treatment of its citizens, and all were restored to their jobs. In January 1992 the Pentecostal church in Riyadh was raided, and five Christians were struck with 50 lashes and held for months.

Customs officials have shredded the personal Bibles of foreign workers entering the country. Some families have been expelled for giving religious instruction to their own children in their own homes. The owner of a Christian bookstore was reportedly arrested, held in prison on a trumped-up charge of prostitution, tortured into signing a confession, and sentenced to 180 lashes and four months in prison. Such religious bigotry and intolerance clearly violates not only human decency and an enlightened conscience but the United Nations' consensus as well.

Some progressive Islamic sects are critical of such religious coercion, but they exert little influence. Islamic countries profess to observe the teaching of the Koran which says that "There is no compulsion in religion" (2:256). Saudi Arabia not only disregards this law but also abstained from the 1948 United Nations *Universal Declaration of Human Rights*' commitment to freedom of religion. A Saudi who converts from Islam to another religion is subject to execution—usually by beheading or stoning, sometimes by crucifixion.

During the recent war with Iraq, the Saudi government invited a military coalition to defend the nation against Iraqi aggression. This operation had United Nations sanction, United Nations Security Council authorization, and near-worldwide approval. The United Nations made very strong statements about the necessity to abide by internal laws. Yet during this very war where allied forces shed their blood to defend Saudi Arabia and Kuwait against Iraqi hostility, American military chaplains were required to call themselves "morale officers" and were told to remove their crosses and religious symbols. Allied female personnel were literally kept out of sight. As the war proceeded, the Saudi ambassador to the United States subsequently indicated that American troops in Operation Desert Shield could at least have chaplains, Bibles, and worship services as long as Saudi personnel were not involved.

Something is terribly amiss when 500,000 men and women fight a war for liberty and freedom while at the same time they themselves are denied the very thing they are fighting for—the basic principle of freedom, including religious liberty even for American workers living within Saudi Arabian borders.

Religious Freedom Must Be
Part of New World Order

Talk of a "new world order" is empty political talk unless the basic right of religious freedom is addressed in all nations of the world. Religious intolerance lies at the very heart of the conflict between Israeli, Arab, and Islamic neighbors; between Shiite Iran and Sunni Iraq; between Protestants and Roman Catholics in Ireland; between Muslims and Jews, and Muslims and Christians in Lebanon; between various sects in the old Soviet Empire; and between allied forces and Saudis. Religious rights of some minorities are nonexistent in some countries.

Saudi Arabia is a good place to begin since Muslims at least enjoy religious tolerance in New York, London, and many other countries of the world. Foreign workers in Saudi Arabia, both civilian and military, must be free to worship God in good conscience. They must be allowed to possess Bibles, display religious symbols, and meet as congregations for worship. For over 40 years Aramco employees were granted, quietly and unpublicized, the right to private worship and a Bible for personal use. The Saudis have an eager interest in American technology and technical and managerial personnel.

The U.S. State Department is well aware that Saudi Arabia does not permit public or private non-Muslim religious activities. There are disconcerting reports that the United States imposes on its own employees in Saudi Arabia government religious restrictions that are no less strict than some restrictions imposed by the Saudis. The State Department reportedly has since 1985 directed its employees in Saudi Arabia not to worship with other Christians working there. Arriving personnel are advised not to bring in non-Muslim literature.

In 1988 foreign workers in Saudi Arabia numbered 4 million in a total population of 11 million, that is, 36 percent. Of these 4 million workers, only highly paid people were allowed to bring their families to Saudi Arabia. It is time that the United States link military and/or economic aid—exempting only emergency humanitarian assistance—with insistence on the right of all foreign workers residing in Saudi Arabia to openly practice their religious faith without harassment, persecution, or punishment. It need not be assumed, of course, that all American personnel have spiritual interests. Yet we should insist on the right of foreign workers to bring their families. We should insist on the cessation of inhumane punishment. We should insist on the discontinuance of beheading

69

and crucifixion of citizens or foreigners whose only offense is their religious faith. There is and there should be growing interest in religious freedom issues. We need also to ask if it is right for the United States to vote to elect as president of the United Nations General Assembly a representative of any nation that fails to endorse the *Universal Declaration of Human Rights*.

Saudis Deplore, Exploit Materialism in the West

Incongruously, Saudis who travel sporadically to the Western world tend to think they justifiably reject what they consider its materialistic and technological essence for a superior Islamic tradition. However, when Islamic kings and princes come to the West, they seldom if ever touch the cultural heritage and religious heartbeat of the spiritual West. With almost schizophrenic delight they abandon themselves to the excesses of profligate living, squander petrol fortunes in casinos, and probe the best investment portfolios. Then they return to the Middle East garbed in traditional dress and ready to enforce the strictest Islamic dictates in the name of a superior morality, including a Saudi culture where men are allowed four wives and a woman's testimony does not have equality in courts of law. The practice of polygamy, fortunately, has largely disappeared among younger, better-educated Saudis. Saudi spokesmen have seldom interacted with the West's profound spiritual realities that struggle against the naturalistic and materialistic trends that increasingly shape the public arena. Nor do they evidence a desire to learn what genuine spiritual vitalities exist. Much as they deplore the secular West's materialistic preoccupation—and well they may—they shun dialogue over the history of ideas.

Nor can we smugly and pridefully blame them. True as it is that not a few of the service personnel among the half million American and European soldiers encamped in the Saudi desert entered into deep spiritual commitments, most of them were hardly cultural emissaries of the classic West. Their rock music, uncouth desires, and scorn for Saudi prohibitions touching alcohol, women, and the uninhibited freedom of expression could only confirm the warped Saudi misunderstanding of the quintessent West whose ethical contamination and moral corruption they might understandably wish to avoid.

The tragedy is that little if any important discussion of ultimate realities is under way between those American Christians and Saudi Muslims who share a deep concern over the consequences of technological scientism and theoretical and practical atheism. The respect of some Muslim leaders for Christian spokesmen, moreover, has been reduced by the scandals involving American televangelists.

A government policy that aims mostly to preserve a delicate balance of political interests while it escapes dialogue at the deeper level of human duties and rights has only transitory pragmatic value. Any nation that professes profound dedication to human rights cannot without penalty forever postpone interaction over the most fundamental of all rights, namely, religious liberty.

The Time to Address These Issues Has Come

It is time to address such issues in other countries also. The religious situation in Egypt is a case in point. More Christians live in Egypt—an estimated 10 million—than in any other country in the Middle East. Yet Christian converts from Islam who publicly profess their new-found faith have been arrested, tortured, and imprisoned in an effort to persuade them to recant. Human rights agencies estimate that more than 200 persons remain imprisoned because of their Christian faith. Here, too, sentiment is rising that all foreign aid commitments be suspended until Egypt agrees to religious tolerance as pledged by the United Nations' *Universal Declaration of Human Rights*.

Even the religious situation in Israel calls for a new look. While Reform, Orthodox, and nonreligious Jews are granted full liberties in many nations of the world, not so in Israel. Reform Jews increasingly press the charge of religious intolerance against Orthodox Jews. Should we grant billions of dollars in credit and aid to a nation, even when that country is Israel, if only one branch of religion is officially tolerated? It is time to raise the question of intolerance by Israel's official hard line toward Jews who consider themselves as Reform or Conservative, and as Christian or Messianic Jews.

Jews are told that one cannot be a Jew and receive the same rights as other Jews if one believes in Jesus Christ. In principle, this has remarkable implications for Saul of Tarsus and almost every other person we read about in the New Testament, not to speak of Jesus of Nazareth.

71

Jewish Hostility Toward
Evangelism Is Significant

Another bone of contention is the prevalent Jewish hostility toward evangelism. The State of Israel approves the admission of Christian missionaries only according to the numbers that existed before statehood in 1948. Jewish law, it is said, does not allow belief in Jesus. Anyone who tries to get other Jews to believe in Jesus, it is charged, is bent on the destruction of Jewish identity and culture.

Although many nonevangelical Christians have joined many Jews in recent decades in insisting that Jews have their own covenant-relationship to God quite apart from Christian salvation through the gospel of Jesus Christ, most evangelicals as a matter of conscience consider this a rejection of their faith and the basic unity of the Old and New Testaments. This debate gained new dimensions in November when Rabbi Alexander Schindler, president of the Union of American Hebrew Congregations, called on Reform Jews to define their beliefs and evangelize for Judaism. While this emphasis on the propriety and necessity of evangelism by Reform Jews may perhaps offend some Orthodox Jews, it confers a certain legitimacy also on Christian insistence on the right to evangelize both Jews and Gentiles. There are signs, in fact, that a younger generation of Jews in Israel, discomfited by the existing religious tensions, are more interested than their parents in recovering the Jewish Jesus.

It is noteworthy that in the United States most Jewish converts to Christianity have been Reform Jews. There are between 30,000 and 32,000 Christian Jews in the United States. This does not include many Jews who call themselves Messianic Jews, preferring to be identified more closely with cultural Judaism than with Christianity. At any rate, Jewish believers in Jesus Christ, beginning with the apostle Paul and the apostle Peter, are usually zealous in making Messiah known. After being hauled into civil court for distributing religious literature at airports and in other public places, Jews for Jesus carried their case to the U.S. Supreme Court, where they prevailed and were awarded legal costs totalling $250,000. They have clearly made the point that so-called church/state separation does not make legitimate a restraint of Christian activity that involves free exercise of religion.

This debate has extended even to the postal system, due to the contention of some Jews that Christian materials posted to them constitute obscene and offensive mail.

Political and religious issues relating to Israel must be considered without name-calling. Jews and Christians alike should be able to discuss Israel's occupation of the West Bank and the Gaza Strip without being called anti-Semitic. Criticism of extremist Orthodox religious regulations and restrictions is not anti-Semitic.

China Situation Needs Attention

Of great interest also is the situation in mainland China, both because of the present Communist regime's continuing pressures on house churches and because of anxiety and fear arising from the scheduled reversion of Hong Kong to China in 1997. Congressmen Frank Wolf of Virginia and Chris Smith of New Jersey have indicated personally to Premier Li Peng the concern of some 110 members of Congress over China's persecution and imprisonment of Christians, as well as over the massacre of student protesters. They warned that China's Most-Favored Nation Trade Status could be in jeopardy. President Bush, unfortunately, subsequently vetoed a bill that attached significant conditions to the trade bill.

Urgency of Addressing
Religious Liberty Concerns

The urgent priority of addressing religious liberty concerns in this closing decade of the century and in the years beyond lies in several considerations. Despite the pride of the West in the technological achievements of modernity, religious intolerance and persecution remain besetting evils of much of the contemporary world. The once dominantly Christian West is now sinking into unbridled naturalism, and an atheistic world view often accommodates tyrannical government and a disdain for religion. In the United States itself the constitutional assurance of free religious expression is increasingly subordinated to an exaggerated and distorted emphasis on religious nonestablishment. Militant hostility to the Christian faith remains a concomitant of atheistic communism in China and much modern Koranic religion. Yet for evangelical Christians, the necessity of focusing on concerns of religious freedom, intolerance, and oppression lies rather in something more fundamental; that is, that all humanity bears the creational image of God and is called to worship the Creator "in spirit and in truth." The church of Jesus Christ must be alertly prepared for the possibility that, while others speak of the evolutionary progress of history and a dawning global utopia, this next decade may well witness an outbreak of anti-Christian hostility unprecedented since biblical times. Jesus of Nazareth left no doubt of the inevitability that on this spiritually rebellious planet persecution and even martyrdom would be the lot of His obedient followers. "In the world you shall have tribulation," said Jesus (John 16:33), and we had best take Him at His word. Persecution was a norm to be expected by His faithful disciples. The benign experience of American Christians has been a benevolent exception, providentially enabling their worldwide missionary engagement.

The effort of American evangelicals to penetrate and reshape the culture has been needlessly diluted because secular priorities too much invaded the churches themselves. The entrepreneurial confidence of many leaders of evangelical causes rested less on prayer than on secular fund-raising techniques. The television outreach on which many evangelical evangelists relied for a vast audience recognition and funding became the very instrument that not only publicized the moral weaknesses of some concessive leaders, but it also unfairly stigmatized the whole evangelical witness in the sight of the secular elite. The current recession has resulted in a further decline in giving that has smudged red ink on much of the evangelical enterprise.

If the Anglo-American evangelical movement is to avoid unexpected containment as a modern Essene community in an overwhelmingly pagan society, it will need to relearn that the church of Jesus Christ is engaged in a cosmic spiritual warfare that contains everywhere and always the possibility of demonic attack on the church's witness. The viability of the true church depends on its supernatural life mediated by the Risen Lord, not on promotional ingenuity.

Church Faces Costly Misjudgments

In fulfilling her world mission, the church faces the possibility of two costly misjudgments, both of which can only gratify Satan and his minions. The first danger, to which ecumenical Christianity succumbed, is a dilution of its message into a politico-economic cultural concentration that ignores the biblical gospel of personal regeneration. The second danger is the evangelical concentration on personal evangelism that withdraws from cultural concerns and permits alien forces to shape the public arena, so that the church is marginalized and functions in society only by the tolerance of her foes.

The evangelical community must champion religious freedom for the entirety of humankind, while also welcoming that freedom to proclaim the gospel of free grace worldwide. The earnestness of evangelical commitment to religious liberty, and the full use of it, may be the critical test of the movement's spiritual and moral vitality in an increasingly neopagan society.

If the believing church in the free world does nothing to assist persecuted and oppressed Christians, we fail both Christ and them, because we then yield free course to tyrannical oppressors. We need to name both the victims of religious oppression and their heavy-handed authorities in our private and public prayers. We need to protest discrimination directly to foreign leaders and their embassies in Washington and elsewhere. We ought to press for sanctions against those who routinely violate religious liberty principles. Other than emergency relief and survival assistance, we ought to oppose American financial and military aid to governments guilty of gross human rights violations. We need to publicize through the print and electronic media candid accounts of religious freedom violations. We need to call our own churches to repentance for indifference to the plight of harried spiritual brethren. We need to take an interest in the families of victims of religious oppression, assure them that we suffer empathetically with them, and pray for them. We need to exert lawful pressures on political leaders whose policies on rights issues are more pragmatic than principled.

No less ought we to encourage a depoliticization of foreign policy that allows material and military interests to cancel a deep interest also in human rights and duties and ignores the plight of minorities living in religiously oppressive contexts. It will be no enduring gain for civilization if the West offers the Middle East only a larger exposure to secular materialism and military technology and learns nothing from Islamic interest in a comprehensive spirituality. The way for the West to challenge the alien Islamic world is by a recovery and revelation of its own deep spiritual resources.

The elimination of Saddam Hussein is not the precondition for a just and peaceful world. The basic problem is human nature regardless of culture. Hitler, Hussein, and Khomeini publish the potentialities for evil that are latent in all of us.

Nor are rights self-validating and self-sustaining. Germany was a democracy devoted to equal rights in the generation before Hitler. The problem is basically spiritual and moral. What is at stake is a collision of world views. Political restraints are very important, and we do well to applaud the wearisome effort to postpone hostilities. Such restraints are not absolutely decisive.

Compromise Traps Christianity

The Western world is unfortunately trapped in a costly compromise of its own spiritual heritage. To be sure, it champions compatible social values such as political self-determination, private property, capitalism, and human rights. It eclipses the doctrine of divine judgment, even of divine creation, of sin and redemption, and of the regenerate church as a new society. Secular humanism exploits this vacuum and projects illusory utopias. Meanwhile, the heritage of creedal Christianity is in a cultural free-fall.

Evangelical Christianity, while retaining evangelistic momentum, is nonetheless yielding religiocultural initiative to American Catholicism, especially in influential political, educational, and media sectors. The consequences of such evangelical retirement are twofold. On the one hand there is increasing talk of Catholic-Evangelical cobelligerency in America to confront the rising tide of naturalism, and to do so only or largely on the basis of such broad covering motifs as natural law, common good, and distributive justice. On the other hand, the papal characterizations of evangelical gains in Latin America as deplorable sectarian inroads can only dampen prospects for suitable Catholic-Evangelical cooperation. Meanwhile, more and more observers of the new situation in Eastern Europe are apprehensive over possible ecclesiastical strife between the Eastern Orthodox, Catholic, Protestant ecumenist, evangelical, and other groups. Were such contention to occur, it would seriously challenge the thesis that religious liberty is the best guarantee of a stable society.

Eastern European countries looked with good reason toward the West for democratic and capitalistic alternatives to the socioeconomic controls that plunged them into seven decades of deepening disillusionment. With whatever weaknesses and however imperfectly, the West nonetheless modeled a concern for human rights, religious liberty, private property, and a free market system. Whether the former Soviet empire and new Commonwealth of Independent States can survive the pitfalls of hasty transformation without social chaos remains to be seen. In any event, it is the Christians of Eastern Europe who endured prison rather than capitulation to tyrants, and who look to God and not to material things as the enduring joy of life, who are even now willing to suffer for the proper priorities.

Evangelicals Ought to Be in Forefront

If in the present world a bold insistence on religious liberty is to arise as never before, it is the 35 million adult, born-again Christians in America who ought now to take the lead by way of gratitude for their own inheritance and experience. If we in the West, and particularly in America, lose this opportunity to reverse the naturalistic tide, it will be devout Eastern Europeans who will be setting the example and teaching us. They have experienced the fragility of culture and know that losing a culture is not the same as losing God. Losing God is what we have most to fear. If we lose Him we shall inevitably lose the culture also, and ourselves as well.

Notes

1. World Christian Encyclopedia (Nairobi: Oxford University Press, 1982), 5.
2. *Ibid.*
3. Herbert Schlossberg, *A Fragrance of Oppression: The Church and Its Persecutors* (Wheaton, Ill.: Crossway Books, 1991), 51.

7

Reacting to the Needs of the Nation

By Roy T. Edgemon

I would like to do four things in this chapter. First, I would like to look at how God deals with nations in the Bible. Second, I want to look at the beginning of our nation. Third, I want to look at our nation today. And fourth, I want to examine the call for discipleship.

How God Dealt With Nations in the Bible

It is surprising how much the Bible is devoted to how God deals with nations. The God who notes the fall of the little sparrow is also very much concerned with the lives of all people and nations. We read in the Bible: "Blessed is the nation whose God is the Lord; and the people whom He hath chosen for his own inheritance" (Ps. 33:12). The Bible also says, "Righteousness exalteth a nation: but sin is a reproach to any people" (Prov. 14:34). And, "Except the Lord build the house, they labour in vain that build it: except the Lord keep the city, the watchman waketh but in vain" (Ps. 127:1). The fourth verse is "If my people, which are called by my name, shall humble themselves, and pray, and seek my face, and turn from their wicked ways; then will I hear from heaven, and will forgive their sin, and will heal their land" (2 Chron. 7:14). The last verse is found in the writings of Daniel, "And he changeth the times and the seasons: he removeth kings, and setteth up kings; he giveth wisdom unto the wise, and knowledge to them that know understanding" (Dan. 2:21).

God has all eternity to deal with individuals and their sins, but I do not believe this is true concerning nations. If a person sins against God and lives in rebellion, he sometimes can apparently prosper right to the grave without ever meeting the judgment of God. God has all of eternity to deal with that person. I do not believe this is true with a nation. Nations do not exist as nations in eternity. If God is going to judge a nation, then He must do it during the existence of that nation on earth. If God is going to judge Nineveh, Tyre, Egypt, and Babylon, then He must do so during the existence of those nations. We find in the Bible that this is exactly what God did.

We see all through the Bible that God does judge nations, and therefore, holds Christians responsible for the acts of those nations.

In the days of Isaiah, the proud and haughty nation of Assyria invaded tiny Judah. Rabshakeh stood and shouted blasphemies against the name of the God of Israel. The people quaked with fear. Godly King Hezekiah took the letter that Sennacherib had written, called for the prophet of God, and went into the temple. He bowed upon his knees, spread the letter before the Lord, and made intercession for a nation. He said, "Lord, what must we do?" That night God sent an angel—just one angel—and 185,000 Assyrian soldiers were destroyed (2 Kings 19). God responded to the needs of a nation.

The entire Book of Jeremiah is a call for a nation to repent and come back to God. In the Book of Ezekiel, we find that God was looking for a man to stand in the gap for the nation. In the Book of Amos, we find God pronouncing judgment not only upon the surrounding nations, but upon the covenant nation of Israel as well. We find in the Book that God is very much concerned about sin in the lives of the leaders of a nation and about corruption in high places.

Do not tell me that religion and politics do not mix! God mixed them long ago! God expects Christians to react to the needs of their nation. Even today, God is looking for men and women who will stand in the gap in our land.

In the New Testament, we find our Lord standing in the temple area and crying to a wayward nation, "O Jerusalem, Jerusalem, thou that killest the prophets, and stonest them which are sent unto thee, how often would I have gathered thy children together, even as a hen gathereth her chickens under her wings, and ye would not" (Matt. 23:37).

Because God is concerned about all nations, He is concerned about our own country.

A Look at Our Nation in the Early Years

It is helpful to look back to the founding of our great nation. On that autumn day in 1620 when the little group of brave men and women boarded the *Mayflower* for a strange and distant land, they set sail with faith in God in their hearts. Many days later, just before they landed in the New World, the Pilgrims drew up and signed the "Mayflower Compact," a document based upon their interpretation of the Bible and a document that has been described as "the birth certificate of American democracy."

In the years that followed, such great schools of our nation as Harvard, Yale, Princeton, and Columbia were founded on these same principles. These schools were founded for the purpose of training students for Christian leadership. They were founded to train people to reach others for Christ. An early motto of Harvard was "For Christ and the Church."

In the 1700s, those remarkable men who emerged as the leaders of our country pledged their sacred honor, and a nation was born. Many of these men were believers in God. There seems to be a movement today to debunk our Founding Fathers and make light of those who were instrumental in the founding of our nation. I saw where a handwriting analyst had accused Benjamin Franklin of forging most of the signatures on the Declaration of Independence! Another "handwriting expert" who had studied these signatures reported that 20 of the men were scared and signed their names with great fear and timidity. I wonder if the handwriting analysts have ever read of what happened to those men who signed this sacred document? When Charles Carroll signed, he wrote in bold letters "Charles Carroll of Carrollton" to make sure his signature was not mistaken for someone else with the same name. This does not sound like the jitters to me. These men knew what they were doing. They were responding out of their faith and pledging their lives and all that they had.

80

As I think of our nation in those early years, I see in my mind George Washington kneeling on the ground at Valley Forge in the bitter winter of 1777, like Hezekiah of old, making intercession for his country. Washington later said to the American people in the first speech he made as president, "The propitious smiles of heaven can never be expected on a nation that disregards the eternal rules of order and right, which heaven itself has ordained."[1]

A Look at Our Nation Today

We live in a great nation today. There is much that is good in our country, but there is much that is bad in our land. America has sinned against God. The words of Christ to the church at Laodicea apply to our nation in 1992: "Because thou sayest, I am rich, and increased with goods and have need of nothing: and knowest not that thou art wretched, and miserable, and poor, and blind, and naked" (Rev. 3:17). Southern Baptist editorial cartoonist Jack Hamm once did a drawing of the Statue of Liberty. The woman stood with head bowed; the torch had been dropped to her side; there were tears running down her face. The caption over the drawing read, "It's late, America."

The late historian Arnold J. Toynbee wrote, "The problems that have beset and worsted other civilizations have come to a head in our world today."[2] I say that nowhere is this more apparent than in the United States. Evangelist Billy Graham told a radio audience that we are facing the fourth great crisis of our nation, the other three being the Revolution, framing of the Constitution, and Civil War. The fourth is the spiritual crisis that we face in our world today.

Crime and violence run rampant in our nation. I know a person can walk down the streets of Tokyo; throughout the country of Singapore; in Madrid; and in Seoul, Korea, absolutely confident that no one is going to accost him or her unless it is some crazed maniac. This cannot be done in any large city in America. According to the latest FBI figures, motor vehicle thefts occurred at the rate of 771 per 100,000, while the incidence of assaults was 435 per 100,000. Living in our cities can be hazardous to our health.[3]

The media of movies and literature have created moral cesspools which have inundated the American people with mind pollution. How far we have fallen can be seen in the recent charge by a university professor that people who object to pornography are basically anti-intellectual.[4]

Sin is terribly funny today to the American people. We are giggling and laughing our way straight into hell. There is a cynicism about integrity—from the White House and Capitol Hill to the county courthouse and backyard fence. We are living in a day when national figures can unashamedly live in adultery and say, "I have done nothing wrong."

Some say that the greatest sin in America is indifference, that we are a people who do not care. In 1989 we spent a total of $264.4 billion on various forms of recreation.[5] Americans pay as much for pet food every 52 days as we spend on foreign missions in a year.[6]

Instead of simply cataloging the sins of America, I am going to name some institutions and persons who have contributed to our current condition and failed to stem the tide of sin.

The courts of our land have failed. Decisions have been made in our lifetime by our courts, the Supreme Court in particular, that have moved our nation farther away from God and, in my opinion, away from the dream of the Founding Fathers.

The schools have failed. The philosophy of humanism is not sweeping across our school systems today; it is already firmly entrenched. Along with it there is a spirit of subtle atheism prevalent on many campuses. Those who hold an evangelical position are held up to ridicule in many schools.

Many churches have failed. We are told that in the Southern Baptist Convention, 70 percent of our churches are either losing membership or are at a state of plateauing, and that is from a five-year study, not just what happened in a particular year.[7] Something is wrong with our churches. Someone has said that you look for the church and find it in the world, and you look for the world and find it in the church. I wonder about the churches today when I read about the growth of the early church and the spread of Christianity throughout the Greco-Roman world. In writing of the rapid spread of Christianity in the third century, Tertullian wrote: "Men proclaim that the state is beset with us. Every age, condition, and rank is coming over to us. We are only of yesterday, but already we fill the world."[8] Are we salt and light in our world today? Are we serious about our commitment to a living Savior? In some places the American pulpit has become the vast wasteland. It seems that poor, pitiable, powerless preaching has become the rule rather than the exception.

The American home has failed. We have many houses but few homes. There is an emptiness in the American home today and as a result homelife is crumbling. Children in many homes are regarded as a burden, not a blessing.

The basic problem of our day has been summed up by Will Durant, one of the highly respected philosopher-historians of the last generation. He writes: "The greatest question of our time is not communism versus individualism, not Europe versus America, not even the East versus the West; it is whether humans can bear to live without God. Can civilization hold together if man abandons his faith in God?"[9] This is our basic problem. We, like the prodigal son, have taken our inheritance and gone into the far country. We have sown the wind and now we are reaping the whirlwind. I pray that what T. S. Eliot wrote will not be our epitaph: "And the wind shall say, 'Here were decent, godless people: Their only monument the asphalt road and a thousand lost golf balls.'"[10]

Where Do We Go From Here?

I am grateful to God that the word *man* in the Greek language is the word *anthropos,* which means "the one who looks up." The answer to our needs today is to look to God. Edward Everett Hale, former chaplain of the United States Senate, said, "I am only one, but still I am one. I cannot do everything, but still I can do something; and because I cannot do everything I will not refuse to do the something that I can do."[11]

A Plea for Participation

What can we do as churches and leaders of those churches? I believe from the depth of my heart that one of the problems we are facing in America is the lack of discipleship, that we have not discipled our people.

In 1978 Jesse Fletcher was preaching at the Southern Baptist Convention. This is the way he started his message: "It is my conviction that our crisis is not in evangelism but in discipleship."[12] That was the first year our evangelism had fallen below 400,000 and had begun to drop further. Fletcher continued, "Evangelism is a by-product of discipleship, not the other way around. . . . I believe our discipleship crisis is caused by a failure to understand the hope of our calling. Too many baby Christians know they belong to Jesus Christ, but they don't know what happens next. They have been told to wait for His coming, but they do not understand the meaning of the in-between time."[13] That is the failure that we have in America today.

Pursuit of Participation

Evangelicals, through *Christianity Today*, employed the research of Win Arn, the church growth specialist, at Fuller Theological Seminary. He looked at back-door evangelism; that is, why do so many people come through the front door and leave by the back door? We, as Southern Baptists, have perhaps one of the worst records in all of the world. We have 15,385,000 Southern Baptists who are members of our churches. Only 50 percent of those were active–that is, attending at least one service–last year. That counts all of those who came on Easter, all of those who came on Mothers' Day, and all of those who are one-timers. Twenty percent of our resident active membership did not attend at all during last year. Thirty percent of our membership cannot be found.

Win Arn said, "An evangelistic process that sees as its goal a 'decision' rather than a 'disciple' tends to create dropouts. Effective evangelism sees disciple-making as a process, not an event. A 'decision' is only one element of many in the goal of seeing people become disciples and responsible church members."[14]

Dietrich Bonhoeffer wrote, "Disciples are the highest good, the supreme value which the earth possesses and without them it cannot survive. Disciples are the salt that sustains the earth."[15] The community of disciples must be faithful to the mission which the call of Christ gave it.

Everyone who responds to the call of Jesus Christ is the salt of the earth. In our total existence, in every thought and action, we are the salt of the earth. There are no options. This salt is not something we have, or use, or might become. It is who and what we are. As it is what we are, it is also what we do. Our mission from our Lord is to save and change the world. If we cease to perform that mission or fail to live up to that mission, our purpose is gone, our direction is aimless, and our identity is blurred.

At the same time, Jesus pronounced that we are not only the salt of the earth, but we are the light of the world. Then and now the beliefs, perspectives, attitudes, and actions of disciples are to distinguish them from the rest of the world and reflect the glory He gives us as He lives inside of us.

Therefore, we, the church of Jesus Christ, are in a unique and appointed position to be salt and light in the political and governmental arenas of this nation. However, at times it seems that the salt has lost is savor and the light has been hidden.

Positioned for Participation

In his book, *The Frog in the Kettle*, George Barna explains the current lack of visibility and influence of the church. He asserts that one of the glaring weaknesses of the church has been in the area of discipling and accountability. Without discipleship and accountability there is no salt and there is no light. Barna insists that in the 1990s the church must confront spiritual crises by leading believers to disciple other believers.[16]

The entire point of this book is moot unless our churches and church members immediately take seriously the discipline of discipleship. Short of proactive discipleship, there is no hope for church members significantly to impact culture, government, or politics.

Be More Than Citizens

There is a danger here. We might get people more involved in citizenship, but simply being an informed and involved citizen is not sufficient. A church member who is an informed and involved citizen is dangerous to the cause of Christ unless that church member is discipled to follow Jesus Christ and is, in turn, discipling others. Fifty years ago Dietrich Bonhoeffer warned the Nazi Christians and recognized the relationship between discipleship and spiritual influence when he wrote, "Christianity without the living Christ is inevitably Christianity without discipleship, and Christianity without discipleship is always Christianity without Christ."[17]

Our nation was founded on the assumption of Christian, traditional values and strength of those citizens who held these values. The framers of the United States Constitution relied on these precepts and participants in government as the infrastructure of that document. In today's pluralistic and secular society where Christian influence is all but absent from politics and government, the interpretation of the Constitution is jeopardized because it is out of cultural context. We can only inter-

pret the Constitution in the context of the Christian values of
the men who wrote it.

Thus, it is imperative for Christian disciples to shape their
culture. Nineteenth-century political analyst Walter Bagehot
evaluated the United States Constitution as "a relatively confused instrument of government" which would "invite chaos
and the crafty manipulation of government by backstage oper-
ators." He concluded that the secret to America's success was
not the Constitution itself, but the quality of the people who
live under the Constitution.[18]

One of the books that has affected my life in the past year
is Stephen Covey's book on *Seven Habits of Highly Effective
People*. This is a book on leadership. Covey, in his study as a
professor, went back to look at all of the leadership of the last
200 years in America. His conclusion was that during the first
150 years American leaders were principle-driven; during the
past 50 years they are personality cults, and that we have lost
the concept of having principle-driven leaders.[19]

Permeate Society

We must permeate society with those values that were
given to us by the framers of the Constitution. When framing
the United States Constitution, the authors did not anchor the
human rights of freedom and liberty in the image of God. The
Fathers of the Constitution entrusted its power to citizens who
subscribe to traditional values. They did not provide for the
operation of the Constitution in a culture which no longer
respects those values. That is the problem we face today.

Unfortunately, therefore, the door is open to manipulation
by those who seek personal gain and ungodly ends. No instrument of protection operates automatically—the responsibility
rests on Christian citizens to be salt and light at every level of
government and politics if we expect our society to reflect
Christian values. How can you and the individual members of
your church be salt and light in America today?

What Can the Church Do?

What can we do as a church? First of all, I think we need
to recognize something that John Naisbitt says is happening.
One is to recognize that our people are sick and tired of our
government. They are tired of the way it manipulates; they are
tired of what it does. Naisbitt observes that Americans are

growing weary of a democracy controlled by the political elite. He predicts that the ethic of participation will change the political landscape in America in the next decade because people who are affected by a decision want to be involved in the process of arriving at that decision. This unwillingness to be controlled by a few powerful representatives leads Naisbitt to believe that America is approaching a shift from a representative democracy to a participatory democracy.[20]

As participatory democracy becomes more prevalent, citizens will have more authority in government. With increased authority comes increased responsibility. The hearts of the people must be prepared for this role by evangelizing and discipling people at all levels of our society.

Local Southern Baptist church government is a microcosm of responsible democracy and thus provides apt training for effective citizenship. If our people can operate in that church, surely we can operate in our local and national governments.

Increase Spirituality

We must lead the call and challenge for spiritual awakening. I am grateful for churches that are participating in prayer for spiritual awakening. We do have 1,700 churches that are praying one hour out of every 24 hours. That means right now 10 churches are praying for spiritual awakening in America. We asked them not to pray for sickness, not to pray for the needs of the local church in the sense of ill people or things that might be happening, but to pray for one thing: spiritual awakening. If spiritual awakening comes to America, we will be making a tremendous contribution to changing this government.

Develop Responsibility

We need to help develop a responsibility as disciples and a responsibility as citizens to government. Garrison Keillor, famed radio storyteller, gives weekly reports from Lake Wobegon, Minnesota, his fictional hometown. One week he said that Father Emil, the Roman Catholic priest in Lake Wobegon, had written a letter to Washington suggesting the construction of a Statue of Responsibility on the west coast since there is a Statue of Liberty on the east coast, and therefore have a balance between liberty and responsibility. Keillor noted that responsibility is a valued virtue in Lake Wobegon.

Even the Catholic church there is named Our Lady of Perpetual Responsibility.

Sadly, however, Lake Wobegon is not typical of American communities. Responsibility and ownership in politics is frequently reserved for the political elite. Average Americans do not feel responsible for government because they feel powerless to influence it. They have no ownership of the process or outcome.

Change Attitudes

Another challenge facing the church as it prepares responsible and involved Christian citizens is to change the attitudes of citizens toward politics and government. Without politics, group decisions cannot be reached. Politics needs to be recognized as a "healthy and necessary part of social life."[21] Therefore, churches should teach and preach that unethical politics is a deviation which should be resisted, challenged, and changed by informed, committed, and active Christian citizens who take seriously their discipleship under the Lord Jesus Christ.

To prepare Christians for participation in government, churches must train leaders to assume responsibility in the community. Average citizens need to be motivated and willing to exercise proactive leadership in the public realm. Churches can take on politics as a mission. They can form task forces and prayer ministries to orient church members to recognize places of service in government. They can assist Christians in discovering channels of being salt and light in society.

Principles of Participation

What else can we do as individuals? First of all, we can follow the commitment of Christ. As a young Christian, the most influential book outside of the Bible in my life was Charles Sheldon's *In His Steps*. We should bring back that concept of "What would Jesus do under this circumstance?" We should teach that and get our people to live by that, to follow the command of Jesus to love the Lord with all of our hearts, with all of our souls, with all of our minds, as the first and great commandment. The second is like unto the first, to love your neighbor as yourself. All of these are possibilities where we can help our people to understand the needs of getting involved and live the ethic of the cross.

T. B. Maston, the Southern Baptist leader in ethics, wrote in his book, *The Christian in the Modern World*: "God's first law of life is not self-preservation, but self-sacrifice."[22] Jesus, in John 12:24-26, taught us that "unless a kernel of wheat falls to the ground and dies, it remains only a single seed. But if it dies, it produces many seeds. The man who loves his life will lose it . . . whoever serves me must follow me" (NIV). We must educate Christians and guide them to serve.

We must help them to realize that we are the mediating value system of our society. The state is assuming functions formerly exercised by the church, but the church is the essential mediating institution in society. It generates and maintains values. If the church neglects its role, the state has "an unchallenged monopoly on the generation and maintenance of values" in our land, and we have failed our God.

Thus, a priority of the church in the 1990s should be to set and cultivate Christian values. Disciples are the key. If disciples who hold Christian values exercise leadership in community, political, and governmental realms and allow their values to be visible and powerful, the church will regain its role as generator and maintainer of values.

What can we do in our local church in an immediate way? I think these things are absolutely critical. First, I am against abortion, and I am concerned about it, but I am just as concerned by the stillbirths of people who come to our churches and try to get saved, and we do not give them spiritual counseling. We have committed a sin against them. We have taken away their birthright, and we have committed a sin against the Kingdom of God. Every Baptist church in America ought to have spiritual counselors and use a counseling room for those who make decisions. It is not right to try to counsel people in three verses of a hymn. They should be taken aside and trained.

There is another thing about harvest here. If we ever got ready for revival, God might give us one. Right now if we had the thousands saved, what would we do with them? Would we treat them as we do the individuals who join our churches today?

Second, what are we going to do with new-member training? Do they learn their faith by osmosis and rubbing up against enough Christians so that they will begin to take on the values of the Christian life? I was saved out of paganism as a 15-year-old boy. When I came into that church for the very first time and heard the gospel, I had picked up my value system like one picks up germs off the street. My value system was totally skewed, and I had to have somebody to teach me the value system of Christ. What kind of new-member training are we giving those who come into our churches? Our "Survival Kit for New Christians" is now in 130 languages and in very basic English that can be used in any prison in America today.

Third, what kind of balanced curriculum are we giving our people to grow in the Lord? I know we make a lot of fun of giving parts, but I want to tell you that giving parts in a Training Union program is what gave me the value system and doctrine of my faith. What are you substituting for that? It is still some of the best literature in all the world.

Fourth, we need doctrine studies—the doctrines of the Lordship of Christ. This year's annual Baptist doctrine study of the Bible is the most widely accepted book on any doctrine that we have had in years. We have 17 leaders in Southern Baptist life, theologians, who have said, "If that is what you mean by inerrancy, I buy it. If that is what you mean by interpreting the Bible, I believe it." I have taught this all over America, and I have yet to have one person come up and say that David Dockery made a mistake and is wrong in the way he did that doctrine. Instead, they have said this is what will bring us together. This is what will unify us around our understanding of the Bible that we hold so dear.

MasterLife is now in over 120 countries all over the world. MasterLife changes people's lives. Ed Young said at our trustee meeting recently that Second Baptist Church, Houston, has now graduated 2,700 people in that course. He said members of that church are not allowed to do anything in the area of leadership there until they have completed a basic course in what it means to be a disciple.

MasterLife is now in more than 50 state and federal prisons in the United States. We have an open door to get into all of them if we just had enough Christian disciples to be willing to go and lead a study in a prison. Prisoners cannot lead prisoners in any kind of educational situation, so it must be an outsider that comes in. MasterLife is making a difference in the lives of prisoners. If we want to reform our system, and those who are in our penal system, then bring them to Christ and disciple them. It gives them the handles for their lives. When they come out of those prisons, they will be productive people. We're seeing them by the thousands.

LIFE Support Curriculum Helps the Hurting

Then, for the bruised, broken, and bound, our trustees have just given us the okay and budget support to develop a new curriculum called "LIFE Support" to help those who are hooked on drugs, co-dependent, and families of alcoholics. If you see *Modern Maturity* for March 1992, with a different kind of cover for that AARP magazine, it says in big bold letters, "11 million Americans hooked on alcoholism." Then underneath it says in the same size bold letters, "That means 76 million family members affected by those 11 million alcoholics." We are living in a bruised and battered world. Jesus taught us in Luke 4 that He came to set free those who were bound and heal those who are bruised and broken. This new curriculum will come out this summer. One of the first courses that will come out is "Making Peace with your Past," which will help people begin to understand why they hurt so. Others will be Robert McGee's "Search for Significance" and "First Place," a wholeness program of Christian health that comes out of First Baptist Church, Houston. These are some of the things we can do.

I want to quote from the 30th anniversary issue of *Christianity Today* dated October 17, 1986. The whole issue was reflecting on the magazine's impact on American evangelism. It closes with an editorial which is the only part of that magazine that looked ahead. It challenges us by saying that if we do not learn how to win the cities, we are not going to learn how to win the world. We do not know how, so we must learn how to win the cities. "The greatest challenges of the church during the next 30 years, therefore, are the need for both evangelization and discipleship. We are surrounded by a materialistic, self-centered, pleasure-seeking society of individuals. As Christian witnesses, we must enter that environment to reach the lost. To the degree that we are successful in introducing them to the Savior, our task of discipleship becomes all the more urgent. It will be wonderful to fill our churches with new believers. It is equally important to nurture them in the faith. If we win the battle for evangelism, but lose the battle for discipleship, we have lost the church of the next generation."[23]

Discipleship training from the very beginning, growing, developing the people of God is not an option, and it is a sin if we don't do it.

Notes

1. George Washington. First Inaugural Address, 1789.

2. Arnold J. Toynbee, *Civilization on Trial* (New York: Oxford University Press, 1948), 27.

3. U.S. Federal Bureau of Investigation, *Crime in the United States*, annual, reported in *Statistical Abstracts of the United States*, 1991 (Washington, D.C.: U.S. Department of Commerce), 176.

4. For a discussion on the loss of a moral consensus in the United States, see Mark Noll and David Wells, *Christian Faith and Practice in the Modern World* (Grand Rapids: Eerdmans, 1988), 273.

5. *Statistical Abstract of the United States*, 1991, Washington, D. C., 231.

6. Ralph D. Winter, "Reconsecration to a Wartime, Not a Peacetime, Lifestyle" in *Perspectives on the World Christian Movement* (Pasadena: William Carey Library, 1981), 816.

7. *Southern Baptist Handbook* (Nashville: Sunday School Board of the Southern Baptist Convention, 1992), 18.

8. Tertullian, quoted by Will J. Durant in *Caesar and Christ, The Story of Civilization*, vol. 3 (New York: Simon and Schuster, 1944), 603.

9. Will J. Durant. Cited in *12,000 Religious Quotations*, edit and comp. Frank S. Mead (Grand Rapids: Baker Book House, 1989), 171.

10. T. S. Eliot, "Choruses from the Rock," *The Complete Poems and Plays 1909-1950* (New York: Harcourt and Brace, 1952), 103.

11. Edward Everett Hale, quoted by John Bartlett, *Familiar Quotations*, 15th and 125th Anniversary Edition (Boston: Little, Brown and Co., 1980), 590.

12. Jesse C. Fletcher, "The City of God—The Hope of His Calling," *The Christian Index*, June 15, 1978, 6.

13. *Ibid.*

14. Win and Charles Arn, "Closing the Evangelistic Back Door," *Leadership*, Spring Quarter, 1984, 26.

15. Dietrich Bonhoeffer, *The Cost of Discipleship* (New York: Macmillan, 1949), 129.

16. George Barna, *The Frog in the Kettle* (Ventura, Calif.: Regal Books, 1990), 111, 123.

17. Bonhoeffer, 65.

18. Walter Bagehot, quoted by Mark Noll, *One Nation Under God* (San Francisco: Harper and Row, 1988), 193.

19. Stephen R. Covey, *The Seven Habits of Highly Effective People* (New York: Simon and Schuster, 1990).

20. John Naisbitt, *Megatrends* (New York: Warner Books, 1982), 160.

21. Richard E. Gross and Thomas L. Dynneson eds., *Social Science Perspectives on Christian Education* (New York: Teachers College Press, Columbia University, 1991), 58.

22. T. B. Maston, *The Christian in the Modern World* (Nashville: Broadman Press, 1952), 136.

23. *Christianity Today*, October 17, 1986.

Bibliography

Barber, Benjamin R. *Strong Democracy: Participatory Politics for a New Age*. Los Angeles: University of California Press, 1984.

Barna, George. *The Frog in the Kettle*. Ventura, California: Regal Books, 1990.

Berger, Peter L. and Richard Neuhaus. *To Empower People.* The American Enterprise Institute For Public Policy Research, 1977.

Bonhoeffer, Dietrich. *The Cost of Discipleship.* New York: Macmillan, 1949.

Covey, Stephen R. *The Seven Habits of Highly Effective People.* New York: Simon and Schuster, 1990.

Grant, Daniel R. *The Christian and Politics.* Nashville: Broadman Press, 1968.

Johnson, John Warren. *Political Christians.* Minneapolis: Augsburg, 1979.

Noll, Mark. *One Nation Under God.* San Francisco: Harper and Row, 1988.Oxnam, G. Bromley. *The Ethical Ideals of Jesus in a Changing World.* New York and Nashville: Abingdon-Cokesbury, 1941.

Smith, Timothy L. *Revivalism and Social Reform.* New York and Nashville: Abingdon Press, 1957.

8

Whose Church Is It Anyway?

By Cal Thomas

I am a layperson. I have never been to a seminary or walked on the grounds of one, if that's what they do there. I've never had hands laid on me or anything. However, I think the Lord has opened up a tremendous door for me in what I call the "final frontier of evangelism," the press.

In the church of Jesus Christ, we have some problems of definition that are culturally derived. At the end of the worship service the pastor gives an invitation and people walk the aisle. Then they fill out a card. Apparently in Baptist doctrine, God has a Rolodex and has to keep everybody straight on these cards. The pastor makes the announcement, "Johnny's come forward to surrender for full-time Christian service and to go to the mission field," and a thousand "amens" rocket off the wall. Then the pastor sees another card and says Mary has come forward to announce that she believes God is leading her into law, business, journalism, or into the most endangered species we have—to be a homemaker. The response is usually, "Well, good for her."

The message that comes out of this very subtly is that somehow God is more pleased with somebody going into something called full-time Christian service. In my view, it is either all full-time Christian service or it is not Christian service. My mission field is the opinion pages of the nation's newspapers, which I believe is just as valid—not less and not more—than the more classical missionaries.

A Witness to the Press

My wife and I, because of the platform that God has given me in this field, try to witness to some of my colleagues in the press. You think you have it tough—you ought to try these people. It is really a glorious opportunity. We have had some wonderful situations in which to talk with some people, whose names you would know very well and certainly whose publications you would know, about the gospel of Jesus Christ—not about religion and not about Christianity and not about denominations. I tell them with a sense of humor, which tends to break down the resistance and stereotypes, the only denominations I believe in are fives, tens, twenties, fifties, and hundreds. Larry King said to me one night on his show on national television, "Cal, we all know you are very religious, so . . ."

I said, "Hold it, Larry, I used to be religious; now I just love Christ. There is a difference." That was one of the few times in his life that Larry didn't have a follow-up question.

Let me turn my attention to a timely subject—government. There seems to be tremendous frustration in the land now with both the Republicans and Democrats. The opinion polls show that the people's tolerance for and belief in and enthusiasm for their government is at one of the lowest points in modern history. Why is this? Why are people so frustrated?

A primary question here is "What is the function of government?" We ask government to do a lot of things either directly or by neglect, and we wonder why it is not more responsive. I think the reason is that we have forgotten what government was created to do.

In the Declaration of Independence we find the definition of what government was created to do. We are all familiar with Jefferson's flaming phrase, "All men are created equal; that they are endowed by their creator with certain unalienable rights; that among these are life, liberty, and the pursuit of happiness. . . ." In the next sentence this intellectual giant of the American government outlined his understanding of the

95

foundational principle of government. He wrote, "That to secure these rights, governments are instituted among men."

These are the rights that God has endowed. Though not all were personally believers in Jesus Christ, the Founders understood that men and women were flawed, that men and women were sinners, and if they would not be constrained from within by the power of God, they had to be restrained from without by the power of the state acting as God's agent. Now that's what we have gotten away from.

We Forget Humanity's Flaw

We've gotten away from a foundational understanding of the flawed nature of men and women. We pretend now that men and women are basically perfectible because we are basically good. We think if we could just send everyone to the right schools and get them in the right environment, then we could have peace on earth, goodwill to men. If you don't think so, look at the response to Mikhail Gorbachev, the "secular messiah," *Time* magazine's man of the decade. Here was the great human hope for all humankind. This is the one the world had been looking for. He was capable, all by himself, of ushering in the new world order, and yet, in the blink of an eye, he was gone.

So, government is no longer fulfilling the function it was designed to do, and that's why it isn't working. That's very simple and very direct, but that is the answer. It doesn't take someone with a Ph.D. or a Th.D. to figure it out. If we just examine history and examine the dysfunctional nature of government these days, we can see that something is clearly amiss.

During debates I am frequently asked whether I believe the Bible is literally true. My reply is always the same: It depends on what you mean by *literal*. If you mean that because the Bible says we are to be the salt of the earth that that means I think we are all made out of sodium chloride, well, no, I don't believe in that kind of literalism. If you mean by *literally true* that God had enough strength left over after creating everything there is to be able to cause people to write words down accurately so that lost souls could find their way to Him, yes, I believe in that kind of literalism. That's a whole new definition of inerrancy.

Does not logic suggest that if God exists objectively (and He either does or does not, there is no third way) and if He, in fact, sent His only Son to die for sinful humans in the greatest act of love ever demonstrated (so great, in fact, that it has become the definition of love), that such a God would not, indeed, could not, send us an instruction Book that is full of errors?

Would Ferrari deliberately falsify or leave open to interpretation the operating manual of an F-40, which is a car that sells for six figures? Not if he wanted to sell any cars, and not if he wanted to avoid the wrath of customers who had invested such a large amount of money in them.

God's Book Is Without Error

God's priceless investment in humanity has caused Him to convey to us a Book without error in matters touching the nature of God, the nature of humans, the manner by which the gulf between humans and God may be bridged, proper relationships between human beings, history, the means of Creation, and accurate prophecy of what is yet to come.

Those who recoil from such an idea do not fully understand the character of God. They are embarrassed by God. They are not comfortable unless their minds give a twist or a spin to a biblical truth, even if that twist or spin makes out the Bible to be a lie and places humans in the place of God, which was the first sin that led to all the others, including my own.

This departure from the Word of God has led to a power failure in the church of Jesus Christ. It is His church, by the way, not mine or yours. If we want instructions as to how it best operates, we should ask Him and not ourselves or each other.

Many believe we are incomplete without a considerable amount of worldly thinking and so-called wisdom. Some in the Southern Baptist community have been fighting the battle over this for nearly two decades now. The Presbyterian Church (USA) appointed a committee to study human sexuality. The committee's majority report which, thankfully, was voted down at the denomination's convention in Baltimore in 1992, concluded that premarital sex, homosexual practice, and even adultery could be permitted in certain circumstances under a new ethic called "justice-love."

The failure to believe God's Word as sufficient and complete is one of two major factors I believe is responsible for the lack of power in the modern church. The other is biblical illiteracy brought on not by the fact that people *can't* read, but that they *don't* read the Bible. A recent Gallup Poll found that only 17 percent of Americans read their Bible daily.[1] I read mine every day, along with the *New York Times* so that I know what each side is doing!

Biblical Illiteracy Leads to Ignorance

Biblical illiteracy has led to ignorance, which has led to apostasy, which has led to open rebellion against God and His Word. So much so, in fact, that the various denominations which once knew better are now putting themselves in the place of God. As Charles Stanley has noted, we have moved from little Samuel who said, "Speak Lord, for thy servant heareth," to our present moment in which we say, "Listen Lord, for thy servant speaketh."[2]

A few months ago I wrote a column about this trend in contemporary religious circles, and I cited some of the doings in the Episcopal Church and the Presbyterian Church (USA). I noted the Episcopal gadfly Bishop John Spong, who received 15 more minutes of infamous fame because of his latest book, which claims the apostle Paul was a repressed homosexual. Then I said the following:[3]

> It used to be said of the pietistic that "they are so heavenly minded they are of no earthly good." Surely it must now be said of these "progressives," who are nothing more than heretics and apostates in clerical garb, that they are so earthly minded, they are of no use to heaven or anyone on earth.
>
> The nonreligious might view this as immaterial and of little personal interest, but it is of great cultural significance when the Christian church has lost its moral power and has become a prisoner, rather than a leader and liberator, of the culture.
>
> The church once had power: real power, moral power, spiritual power, the power to not only transform people's lives, but also to heal society's deepest ills. That power, as the history of this and other countries has revealed, is greater than any government, no matter how many points of light it seeks to illuminate on its own.
>
> Three years ago, in an address to the Church of Scotland, British Prime Minister Margaret Thatcher touched on the relationship between a vibrant, doctrinally strong church and a muscular nation: She said, "There is little hope for democracy if the hearts of men and women in democratic societies cannot be touched by a call to something greater than themselves. . . . The truths of the

Judaic-Christian tradition are infinitely precious, not only, as I believe, because they are true, but also because they provide the moral impulse which alone can lead to that peace, in the true meaning of the word."[4]

What moral impulse can a church exert when it conforms itself to the world rather than renewing its principles? Is it God who sets the agenda, or, as the deists believed, did He just start the global ball rolling and then leave us to our own devices?

Repeatedly throughout history, a church that was sound and united in its doctrine addressed the social ills of a society by first spiritually transforming people's inner lives and then helping them find housing, jobs, and offering other assistance to provide for their physical needs.

The ultimate anti-poverty program is a changed life.

1890s Were Difficult Time in America

In 1890, many social conditions in America were worse than they are now. As Marvin Olasky has written in *Policy Review* magazine, "Thousands of orphans roamed the streets. Infant mortality rates were 10 times their present levels. New York Police Commissioner Thomas Byrnes estimated that 40,000 prostitutes worked the city. A survey found 6,576 New York slum families living in tenement 'inside rooms'—rooms without windows facing out, only air shafts, which many tenants used as garbage chutes. Gambling, drunkenness, robbery and murder were more common."[5]

It all changed when platoons of the greatest charity army in American history, armed with Bibles and an evangelical zeal not seen since, took on the cause of reform. They had such names as Olivet Helping Hand Society, Hebrew Sheltering and Guardian Society, and such noneuphemistic ones as Union for Erring Women's Refuge. Erring men were assisted by the Salvation Army and other groups.

It is time for a revolution of the people who have not abandoned sound doctrine. Preachers and theologians who have departed from the Truth must be asked to depart from their churches and seminaries. Church members must stage theological coups to topple those from positions of authority who have ignored God's authority. As the prophet Isaiah wrote, "The grass withers, the flowers fade, but the Word of our God shall stand forever" (Isa. 40:8).

Only such a revolution will revive the Christian church, and only a revived church can bring help, healing, and a desperately needed moral conscience to the nation.

99

That's the kind of intolerant stuff I write in my columns that gets me wonderful letters like the one I am about to share with you.

A Presbyterian minister from a small Iowa town wrote to me after reading that column. He chastised me for not being more open to people, and he specifically mentioned homosexuals. Here is some of what he said, and I think he makes my point even better than I tried to do:

> The modern church has been too afraid to reexamine its values and beliefs in light of modern social realities . . . (a more constructive question would be): How can a modern church reform its principles when it is too frightened to examine the problems and conditions of people living in the real world? . . . Modern society, Mr. Thomas, requires a modern church! Fortunately, all of the issues cited above [and he mentioned homosexuality, marital fidelity, birth control, the infertile and the aged] are currently being studied by a number of responsible and faithful denominations. [I should ask, faithful to what or to whom?] But so long as we follow your prescription of fear and hesitate to interpret God's will in light of modern issues, irrelevance will continue to plague the church.[6]

I wrote him and thanked him for making my point and said I would quote from his letter. He wrote back, further criticizing me for my emphasis on orthodoxy and said that being right about an issue is not always the point, though, of course, he said he didn't think I was right. He said love was more important.

The point is, of course, that without a standard and with a negotiable theology, no one is ever able to say who is right and who is wrong. As to his comments concerning love as the highest ideal, love without sound doctrine is sentimentality. It is not love at all, certainly not in a biblical sense. As my colleague Joseph Sobran has written, "It can be exalting to belong to a church that is 500 years behind the times and sublimely indifferent to fashion; it is mortifying to belong to a church that is five minutes behind the times, huffing and puffing to catch up."[7] Isn't that great?

A Third Letter From Reader

I received a third letter from this Presbyterian minister that is even more revealing. Seeking some kind of "reconciliation," he revealed where he was coming from, though I was never in doubt. He wrote:

> I can and must interpret to the best of my ability the scriptural teaching on every subject. I need to listen for and learn about what is consistent in God's message to the world [The heresy here, of course, is that God is inconsistent.], while trying to determine what is excess baggage left over from the cultural and historical situations of the authors. It is a difficult and joyful task, one of many to which I feel God has led me in the ministry. . . . I take it that you accept the Bible to be the inerrant, infallible Word of God, Mr. Thomas. I do not think that is what the Bible is. I believe that the Bible is the history of peoples' search for and experiences with the eternal God recorded by the frail and imperfect minds and hands of human beings. It is still scripture and still uniquely authoritative, but it is in need of interpretation. . . .[8]

There you have it, the "mother of all heresies."

Other denominations have had similar experiences. Episcopalians have felt this tension. When Barbara Harris was named a bishop, many in the media rejoiced. She believes that it is okay to ordain homosexuals to the priesthood. This is the kind of religion the world is looking for, one that authorizes and offers legitimacy to what the world wants to do. It is comfortable with a faith (though it is not really a faith at all) which validates and vindicates the things of the flesh.

Ordination of a Lesbian
Shows Slide into Apostasy

The Episcopal Diocese of Washington, D.C., recently ordained its first openly lesbian person as a priest. And the slide into deeper apostasy continues.

"Do not be conformed to this world," warned the apostle Paul under the leadership of the Holy Spirit, "but be transformed by the renewing of your mind" (Rom. 12:2).

I said earlier that the church is the property of Jesus Christ. That building you go to on a Sunday morning is not a church. One night when I was sitting in for Buchanan in one of his previous incarnations, a producer at CNN sensed some kind of spiritual spark in me, I guess, because I didn't curse or take the Lord's name in vain in her presence. She asked, "By the way, what are you?"

101

I said, "Tall."

She said, "No, no, no. Where do you go to church?"

I said, "I don't. I am the church."

She said, "Listen, wise guy, what do you do on Sunday morning?"

I said, "Well, depending on how I feel, I get a cup of coffee and go to the bathroom."

So she started to get really exercised. She asked, "When you leave the house, where do you go?"

I gave her an address. She said, "Is there a building there?"

I said, "Yes."

She said, "What's the name on the building?"

I said, "What are you getting at?"

She said, "I want to know what you believe."

I said, "Oh, I am happy to respond to that question. But, you see, if I had given you any of the other information, you would have been able to label me according to your understanding of the label, and I'm not willing to be identified by a label." So, when people say, "What are you?" I say, "I'm just a follower of Jesus Christ." They ask, "What's that mean?" I say, "Oh, well, I'll tell you that."

A reporter for the *Christian Science Monitor* came up to me at the Democratic Convention in 1984 in San Francisco. She clearly believed I was a spy for the Religious Right. She did her whole interview on what I thought the role of the Religious Right and conservatives was going to be in that election. At the end of the interview she said, "By the way, are you born again?"

I said, "What do you mean by that?" She said, "Well, huh, huh . . . you know."

I said, "Yes, I know, but do you know?"

She said, "No, I don't."

I said, "Well then, why would you want to use a phrase in your copy that you don't know the definition of?"

She said, "Would you tell me what it means?"

I said, "I would be delighted. Now, the first thing you need to know is that it was not invented by Jimmy Carter, although the guy's initials were the same!"

Scripture contains stern warnings concerning what happens to a church that abandons the Word of God or seeks to water it down or reinterpret it, which is the same thing because it says we do not believe what God has said, or, in fact, that God said it. A group of theologians met to determine how much of what Jesus is reported to have said He actually said. Well, they could have saved themselves the trouble. He said it all. John tells us so much did He say and do, in fact, that "if they should be written every one, I suppose that even the world itself could not contain the books that should be written" (John 21:25).

One of my favorite films of all time is *Chariots of Fire*. It is one of those rare movies where people fall in love, keep their clothes on, get married, and all that regular stuff. That movie has so many wonderful lines in it. It contains so many integrated concepts of a believer acting out his or her faith. One scene involves one of the central characters leaving a worship service in Scotland. In that scene are Eric Liddel, his father, and Eric's young friend, who is his coach. The young friend is inquiring about God and what kind of God He is. Eric's father remarks, "The Kingdom of God is not a democracy. There's no discussion, no deliberation. There's one right, one wrong, one absolute ruler."

The young person then responds, "A dictator, you mean."

"Aye," says Eric's father, "but a benign, loving dictator."[9] I love that line. I think it's one of the most descriptive phrases of the role and function of God that I have read outside of the Bible. A benign dictator. We think of dictators as Hitler and Stalin. Those certainly were not benign dictators. A benign dictator is something quite different. When you find out a tumor is benign, that's a wonderful piece of news.

Fewer Are Obedient to the Word of God

Fewer of the people in our culture, who should know better because of our history, are listening to this "Benign Dictator" because fewer read, understand, or are obedient to the Word of God. When preachers shy away from the Word of God as authoritative, accurate, and reliable, where are the people to turn and what are they to think?

Richard John Neuhaus, as eminent a thinker as we have today, has written, "The church is not for hire, no matter how noble the intentions of those who would hire it. The church is bound for the Kingdom of God and bound by the Kingdom of God, and to settle for less than the Kingdom of God is to be less than the church of Christ."[10]

103

To betray Christ's Word is to betray Christ because, as W.A. Criswell wrote, "Our Lord is identified with His Word. The incarnate Word, the spoken Word and the written Word are one. To dishonor the incarnate Word we have but to disparage the written Word, ... When we therefore find the mind of Christ in the written Word, we find the mind of the Lord Himself."[11]

Today, there are increasing numbers who are embarrassed by Christ and ashamed to admit that He is part of their lives. They allow Christ to be treated as important to them, but not important to their world.

I heard two announcers on a Washington, D.C. radio station during the 1988 political campaign criticize Pat Robertson, then a candidate. They mentioned another candidate by name. One of the announcers said to his partner, "You know what I like about him?" and he mentioned the other candidate's name.

"What?" said his partner.

"He's religious, too," he observed, "but he doesn't take his faith seriously." I was so startled by the frank honesty that I almost ran off the road in my car.

That's the key phrase. The world will allow you to believe in anything. You can worship toast if you wish. Just don't take it seriously. The church of Jesus Christ has ceased to take Jesus Christ seriously, and that is why we have so little power at the end of the twentieth century.

This is what is so remarkable to me about the flight from biblical truth. The modernists claim to be renovating the church, discarding the old and worn out and bringing in the new. They announce this in order to attract more people to their services, but the people don't come. The churches that are full, the seminaries that are prospering, the pastors who are challenging and instructing congregations in the way and will of Christ are those that are shoring up the old, not leveling it and attempting to build something new on a foundation that is in disrepair.

"Whole tracts of our religion are bare of spiritual passion," wrote theologian P.T. Forsyth. "Christianity speaks the language of our humane civilization; it does not speak the language of Christ. The age, and much of the Church, believes in civilization and is interested in the gospel, instead of believing in the gospel and being interested in civilization."[12]

Yes, the modern church has forgotten its first love. It behaves like a tailor, fitting doctrine to suit the customer. E. B. White used such a metaphor when he said, "People have recut their clothes to follow the fashion. . . . People [have] remodeled their ideas, too—taken in their convictions a little at the waist, shortened the sleeves of their resolve, and fitted themselves out in a new intellectual ensemble copied from a smart design out of the very latest page of history."[13]

Writing in his book, *Against the Night*, Chuck Colson recalls Donald Bloesch's contention that "secularism advances only as orthodoxy retreats. As surely as we yield the ground staked out for the church, the barbarians will advance to claim the terrain." The biblical revelation and the historic confession of Christian truth, says Colson, are "the only bulwark that allows the church to both judge itself and stand fast against the currents of cultural trends."[14]

For years, notes Colson, the slogan of the National Council of Churches was, "The world sets the agenda for the church."[15] This sounds socially relevant, but, in fact, it displaces God, who long ago set His own agenda for His church: obedience.

Now why is all of this important? It is important because of people like me. I was not exposed to sound doctrine until I was nearly 27 years old. I went to a building called church every week, but I wasn't exposed to sound doctrine until I was a young adult. I grew up in a liberal church, the pastor of which later became a leader of the ACLU in North Carolina. That ought to tell you something. If I had heard sound doctrine earlier, I might have committed my life to Christ sooner and been spared many of the hard lessons I had to learn.

Church Leaders Responsible
to God for Stewardship

A pastor, seminary professor, or church leader is responsible to God for his or her stewardship of God's Word. We know the verdict already announced on those who would cause even one of these "little ones" to stumble. That means there is judgment reserved for those who lead people astray by watering down God's Word and not being faithful to it.

The primary responsibility of a pastor, leader, and Sunday School teacher is to preach and teach the Word, in season or out of season, when it is fashionable and when it is not, when it is welcomed or when it is rejected. We are to preach it without fear or favor and without consulting the polls or attempting to placate certain contributors or succumbing to threats from deacons, elders or so-called "influential" members.

Each of us, but especially those in positions of responsibility, has a constituency of one. He is the living God. That does not mean that we ought not to be sensitive to what others say to us. God can, and often does, speak through those who love Him to deliver a message He wants us to hear.

In terms of doctrine, God has said everything He wants to say about that, and it is in His Word, which is without error because it was written by the Holy Spirit, who guarded human instruments from making any mistakes.

Because of apostasy, incarnated in political power and watered-down doctrine, John Neuhaus has said,

> In many of our churches, God's people hunger for the Bread of Life and are too often given the stones borrowed from the deadly power games of the world. Preachers become influence peddlers, and churches are turned into political lobbies which, no matter how successful and how much clout they think they have, are, in fact, pitiful appendages to agendas that are set in the public arena by people who neither understand nor care about the nature and the mission of the church of Christ. The church as a tool is a church of fools.[16]

In *Chariots of Fire* Eric Liddel's father gives his young son sound advice, which I think is germane to each of us. "Eric," he says with fatherly love, "don't compromise; compromise is the language of the devil. Run in God's name, and let the world stand back and wonder."[17]

That is the advice I leave with you. Preach, teach, and witness with the power of the wind of the Holy Spirit of God guiding you and the world *will* stand back and wonder. What's more, many in that world will come forward and be changed forever.

Notes

1. George Gallup, Jr. and Frank Newport, "The Bible Is Still Widely Read and Studied, But Biblical Illiteracy Remains Widespread" (Princeton, N.J.: The Gallup Poll Organization, November 15, 1990).
2. Charles Stanley, as recorded by Cal Thomas from a televised sermon.
3. Cal Thomas, column, Los Angeles Times.
4. Margaret Thatcher, *Wall Street Journal*, May 31, 1988.
5. Marvin Olasky, *Policy Review* 54 (Fall 1990): 2.
6. Private correspondence to Cal Thomas.

7. Joseph Sobran, in a column written for Universal Press Syndicate, 1985.

8. Private correspondence to Cal Thomas.

9. *Chariots of Fire*, original screenplay by Colin Welland, Enigma Productions, 1981.

10. Richard J. Neuhaus (In a telephone conversation on October 15, 1992, Neuhaus affirmed that this was an accurate representation of something he had written, but he was unable to identify the specific work in which it appeared.)

11. W. A. Criswell, *Christ and Contemporary Crises* (Dallas: Crescendo Book Publications, 1972), 45.

12. Peter T. Forsyth, quoted by Charles Colson in *Against the Night* (Ann Arbor, Mich.: Servant Publications, 1989), 97.

13. E. B. White, *One Man's Meat* (New York: Harper Colophon, 1982), 135.

14. Charles Colson, *Against the Night* (Ann Arbor, Mich.: Servant Publications, 1989), 150.

15. *Ibid.*, 36.

16. See footnote 10.

17. *Chariots of Fire.*

9

When Culture Degenerates

By William J. Bennett

The ideals that abound in our culture contribute significantly to the illegal drug problems today. We are spending
some $14 billion at the federal level right now, and probably
another $30 or $40 billion at the state and local level to fight
illegal drug usage. Many of these efforts are smart and well-
intentioned, and some will even have effects. Concerted efforts
by law enforcement and education coupled with treatment can
make a difference. However, for all the good that these may do,
they cannot equal the bad that is done by some basic problems
in our society.

A major problem we face is that for more than two
decades now we have let our cultural norms follow the wrong
ideals. In the 1960s, we adopted new ideals which said:

"Do your own thing."

"If it feels good, do it."

"Different strokes for different folks."

At the time, these seemed like innocuous ideas. They
seemed so tolerant, so open. Yet, these ideals have had a dev-

astating impact on our society. When the young heard these and believed them and acted on them, it was disastrous. No more perfect "Do your own thing" exists than drugs, because if you start to do drugs, soon that is the only thing you will be doing. That is why I believe the "Do your own thing" ideal in our culture today has caused more harm than we can undo with years and years of federal budgets.

Education Expenses More Than Defense

Another part of this formula is education. The price tag for American education this year is $414 billion for elementary, secondary, and higher education. In comparison, the budget for the Defense Department is $270 billion. We do some good with that money. There are some great schools in America. There are some fine teachers and principals. However, too many of our elementary, secondary schools, and now our universities do not know why they exist. They do not know their purpose. This great expenditure of money may do some good and may do some harm, but it cannot undo the greater harm done in the late 1960s and 1970s during the great cultural revolution in this country when it was said that "there is no right curriculum to pass on to children. Let children make up their own. Who are we to pass on to children our idea of a right curriculum? It may be right for us, but it may be wrong for them."

At the bottom of that intellectual challenge to the American schools is a more fundamental one, which is a moral challenge. Moral relativism was the worst, most consequential, and most disastrous teaching of all during the last 20 years. It is the idea that there is no such thing as right or wrong. When we let that concept loose in the country's bloodstream, we really created havoc. We must put that genie back into its bottle. I think too many of us at the time were too diffident. We lacked the confidence to challenge that idea. We thought it was just a fringe concept, but it penetrated many parts of American life. We can spend billions of dollars and create dozens of new government programs to no avail until we eradicate that concept. There are things that are right and wrong, and there are things that our children should learn in American education.

A third part of this formula is the family. Over the past thirty years, it has become fashionable for our culture to poke fun at the family as personified by Ozzie and Harriet. We started saying, "That's gone. That's outmoded. That is no more."

Whether we wanted to do so or not, we have been conducting a social experiment in America. In many American communities we have thrown out all the old rules that made the concept of family work. We said, "Let's have babies, but let's not raise them. Let's remove fathers from the presence of boys, and let's see what happens. Let's put them in environments where there are no men, at least no men of righteousness, no men of goodness. Let's put them in environments where the schools do not teach moral values and where we cannot count on a single parent to teach values. Then let's see what happens." We have now seen what happens, and it is not pretty. It is not attractive.

Strong Families Needed

The answer is not all that complicated. We need families—strong families—that teach values and prepare our children for a full and rich life. We need to stand up for the family, and our government needs to do everything it can to strengthen families. However, the real answer isn't in government. Government can only do so much to strengthen families. The real answer lies in our culture. It lies in our cultural values. Over the next decade, the issue of cultural values will move center stage. At least, I certainly hope it does. If we are honest and face squarely the questions this debate will raise, we can begin trying to make this country a better place for all of us, but especially for our children. After all, they are the future.

Nothing in the Constitution prohibits government officials from writing about these things. We would not have had an abolition movement without faith. We would not have had the end of child labor without faith. We would not have had an America without faith. We certainly would not have had a Declaration of Independence without faith.

A wise teacher at Boston University once said to me, "Religion is a domain that we ignore at our peril." That is right. I taught Reinhold Niebuhr at Harvard in 1969-1971 and did not get any standing ovations for doing it either, but I tried to help my students and colleagues understand that unless we paid attention to the religious dimension, we were missing the point. I still think that's true, and I still think we should persist in doing that.

PART IV

Practical
Application

10

How Christians Make an Impact on Their Government

By Beverly LaHaye

Our nation's history is filled with devout Christian men and women who have made an impact on government. Unfortunately, secular humanists have rewritten this account of our heritage in an effort to sell our nation on the misunderstood idea of "separation of church and state." Even the church has been infiltrated to some extent with the unbiblical idea that religion and politics cannot mix. They believe that Christians should occupy themselves only with "spiritual" things and not "waste" their time on politics.

Early American Christians believed in having an influence on society and got involved in politics. Had they not, we would probably not have an America today—certainly not the same America we are privileged to inhabit. Despite all the myths that secular humanists are trying to sell, the truth is, Christians have been making an impact on our nation's government since the very founding of our nation.

America's Birth Rooted in Christianity

The very birth of America was rooted in Christianity. Pilgrims braved the horrors of a 66-day Atlantic crossing, knowing full well that the journey was so treacherous that their chances of survival were 50-50. Why would they take such risks? All for the sake of the gospel.

For the first time in human history, Christians had the opportunity to build a society based on biblical principles of self-government. More than 150 years later, the Pilgrims' vision for this new land had not been forgotten. On July 2, 1776, after the drafting of the Declaration of Independence, Samuel Adams—known to the British as the "Chief Rabble Rouser" among the colonists—stood up and said, "We have this day restored the Sovereign [with a capital "S"], to whom alone men ought to be obedient."[1] Adams's allegiance was to God as he helped draft the Declaration—the document that explicitly acknowledges the Creator as the source of our rights. Samuel Adams' basis for his political beliefs came from his spiritual convictions. He said, "The rights of the colonists as Christians are best understood by reading and carefully studying the New Testament."[2]

James Madison, the chief architect of the United States Constitution, knew the importance of implementing biblical principles of government into this new nation. Madison studied under one of America's great religious leaders, John Witherspoon.[3] The focus of Madison's studies, curiously enough, was the Hebrew principles of government. Madison said, "We have staked the whole of our political institution on the capacity of mankind to govern themselves according to the 10 commandments of God."[4]

In fact, some of the Founding Fathers went so far as to say that this self-government would not work for a people who did not hold religious convictions. John Adams, the second president of the United States said, "Our Constitution is designed for a moral and religious people. It is wholly inadequate for any other."[5]

Unfortunately, America has been slipping away from being a "moral and religious" people. Just as John Adams warned 200 years ago, we see a crisis in our government. We've watched our nation embrace the murder of its defenseless unborn children simply for the sake of "convenience." We've seen our country subtly and now blatantly accept homosexuality as an alternative life-style. We've watched our society

113

indulge in pornography and obscenity under the auspices of "art," even using our tax dollars. Now school teachers and administrators are handing out condoms to our seventh-grade children.

Over the past three decades, we've seen our nation turn away and scoff at the biblical principles on which our nation was founded. Now it is up to us, as Christians, to restore those principles. It is not a question of *can* Christians make an impact on government, but *will* we? We *must* make an impact because our nation's future is at stake. When you look into your child's innocent eyes, how can you *not* become involved?

So how do Christians make an impact on government? Let me share a few points of action that we all must take to make a difference in our nation.

Voting Is A Way to Make Impact

The first action step is extremely important. It doesn't take a whole lot of time, but it is the very cornerstone of self-government. Still, it seems that every year fewer and fewer people bother to do it. It is called *voting.* Did you vote in the last election? What about the last primary? Or the last city council or school board election? Are you registered to vote?

We live in a time in American history when less than half of the eligible voters actually vote. Only 62 percent of the public is even registered to vote. People aren't voting for a variety of reasons, from apathy to a general frustration with the political process. A lot of people think, "My one vote doesn't matter much, so why bother?" I've got news for you! Your vote does count!

In 1986, an off-year election, Republicans controlled the Senate by a slim margin and lost five conservative senators by almost 50,000 votes. The real scandal is 5 million Christians who voted in the presidential election of 1984 didn't even bother to vote in that 1986 election!

The consequences of this lack of voting allowed Senator Ted Kennedy to become chairman of the powerful Senate Labor and Human Resources Committee, where all abortion bills are handled, and vice-chairman of the Judiciary Committee, which rejected Judge Bork and almost destroyed Clarence Thomas. This would have been different if only 50,000 more Christians had voted.

In 1990 Majority of Eligible Voters Didn't Vote

In the 1990 elections, only 46 percent of eligible voters actually cast ballots in the general election. That means that less than half of eligible American voters determined who would run the country for everyone else. Technically, each vote represented a little more than two people. So if you voted in the 1990 general election, your vote was twice as powerful as it would have been had everyone voted.

Your vote can have even more influence in primary elections. Only a fraction of that 46 percent in 1990 voted earlier in the primaries. That means a tiny fraction of the American people narrowed down the choice for everyone else in the country. The fewer number of people who vote, the more important each vote becomes. So in those local elections where voter turnout is even lower, your vote can make all the difference in the world!

Imagine the influence we, as Christians, could have on the political process if we would educate and mobilize our church members and get them to the polls—especially for the primary elections! The body of Christ in America already has the makings of the largest grass-roots network in the nation, and Southern Baptists make up the largest single Protestant denomination.

It is hard to find a community anywhere in the United States without at least one church. The debates we face today are not Democrats versus Republicans, nor one denomination versus another denomination. The issues come down to the biblical mandate to protect the lives of unborn babies, promote traditional family values in public policy and in our culture, and preserve religious liberty for this next generation. If the Christian community would make these its top priorities, our government would never again be the same. We would no longer see our Congress dominated by elected officials who promote the destruction of the unborn. We as taxpayers, who are called to be good stewards of the finances God has blessed us with, would no longer be funding anti-family groups such as Planned Parenthood, or the perverted and sacrilegious trash from National Endowment for the Arts.

The second action item will move individuals closer to the inner circle of power in our government. We must stay in touch with our legislators by communicating our concerns. Don't elect them to office and then forget all about them. Write to them. Call them. Let them know how you feel about an issue.

How much impact can a letter have? Congressmen and senators know that not everyone is going to send a letter expressing how he or she feels about various legislation. So when a congressional office receives a letter, it is viewed as a representation of many constituents' opinions. Some staffers have said they regard one letter as representing the views of 100 people. Others say 1,000. The bottom line is that those letters do make an impact.

Congress Reacts to Letters

If a House member receives 20 letters from his district on a particular issue, he feels deluged. For a senator, it takes about 50 letters to make a strong statement. Imagine what would happen if Christians in just a few churches in each congressional district sat down for one hour a month and wrote letters to their legislators. The congressmen wouldn't know what hit them. That's a basic component of grass-roots action. And grass-roots action is what makes things change in American politics.

The kind of letter that is most likely to catch a legislator's attention is one that is courteous, well thought out, and backed up with a few facts. Provide him with some strong arguments he can use as talking points to convince his colleagues.

Remember, don't become disillusioned if you can't convince a pro-abortion legislator to become pro-life. However, you may be able to persuade him to support a parental notification or parental consent bill. That is a substantial victory in itself. If you really want to make an impact, you must stick with it. Stay educated on the issues and pressure your congressman when a vote is coming up. Your persistence will make an impact in the long run.

Volunteers Wield Clout, Too

My third recommendation will take a bit more sacrifice of time, but over and over again, people tell me that it is one of the most important things a Christian can do to make an impact on the political system. That is: *volunteering*. Volunteer to work on campaigns—to help the candidate that promotes your convictions. By volunteering, you could help make the difference in whether your candidate wins or loses. Many times volunteers make or break a campaign. In a recent race for state legislature in Virginia, a losing pro-abortion candidate said that he just could not keep up with his opponent's pro-life volunteer support. Many times we Christians are too busy with hobbies and personal entertainment to see the importance of campaign involvement. Yet when the candidate we oppose wins, we're the first to bemoan the results. The importance of volunteering—even just a little—cannot be stressed enough.

If you have worked as a volunteer on a legislator's campaign, you have cultivated a relationship with him. A politician does not forget those who helped him get where he is. Many times congressional leaders will input into their computer the names and addresses of contributors and volunteers so that when one of those supporters writes a letter, he or she is sure to read it personally. Letters from contributors and volunteers carry more weight than others—allowing you to have more of an impact.

The fourth action is what self-government is all about. Consider running for office yourself. Perhaps you're not ready to run for the House or Senate, but there are many opportunities for you to run in your local community. You can run for city council or school board. Many of the attacks on the family today come through our public school system. For example, take Wilde Lake High School in Columbia, Maryland. Last year, the school sponsored a two-day "wellness workshop"—as they called it—for 11th graders. The "workshop" dealt with homosexuality and AIDS. One might expect the speakers would include doctors, experts on the dangers of AIDS. That was not the case. The entire forum was led by two homosexual men and a lesbian who were representing the "Sexual Minority Youth Assistance League," a homosexual group for teenagers. Why would a school feel it necessary to provide such a presentation? The principal and school guidance counselor said that it was needed to respond to the "homophobic" prejudice in the school and provide an outreach—in other words, a recruiting opportunity—to students who believe they are homosexual.

Imagine the impact the Christian community could have if several Christians decided to run for school board in this community and all the churches in the area helped to make sure their congregations made it to the polls on election day. If this happened, I can almost guarantee that the homosexual teen group would never propagandize and recruit in the schools again! Having Christians on the school board will help to protect your children!

Fifth, no matter how many of the first four suggestions you follow, it won't be worth anything if not coupled with *prayer*. We must repent of our lack of past involvement and start praying now—consistently—for our nation. Ten years ago, I became aware that many Christians were not obeying 1 Timothy 2:1-2 where we are told to pray for kings and all who are in authority over us. Far too many did not even know the names of those in authority over them, so how could they fervently and effectively pray?

Concerned Women for America began to distribute the Key 16 list for fervent prayer support. This list required that each person fill in the names of the 16 people in authority positions who would influence laws directly affecting their families. See if you can answer the following for yourself:

(1) Our president
(2) Your two senators
(3) Your congressman
(4) Your governor
(5) Your state senator
(6) Your state representative
(7) The Supreme Court Justices:

Harry Blackmun	William Rehnquist
Anthony Kennedy	Sandra O'Connor
Antonin Scalia	David Souter
John P. Stevens	Clarence Thomas
Byron White	

Too many of our people had to start calling city and state government offices to be able to fill in the names. Our leaders need our prayers, and they should be prayed for specifically by name. They need direction and wisdom from Almighty God!

When you walk through some of the government buildings and monuments in Washington, D.C., notice the inscriptions and artwork that reflect the influence of earlier Christians on our nation. For example:

• The Ten Commandments hang just above the Chief Justice of the U.S. Supreme Court.

• A full statue of Moses, as the great lawgiver of history, stands in the Supreme Court Chamber.

• In the House of Representatives Chamber, God's name appears directly over the Speaker's chair. It is embodied in our motto, "In God we trust."

• The north wall of the Senate Chamber also carries the words, "In God we trust."

Other Christians have gone before us and left their mark. We have benefitted from their work today. In recent years such groups as the American Humanist Association, the ACLU, much of the liberal media, and others have intimidated and misled the American people to accept a doctrine of "separation of church and state" which has led to what Richard John Neuhaus termed "the naked public square." Christians are losing their influence, and our society has greatly suffered because of that. I fear what the next generation will inherit from us.

In all of our nation's wars combined, from the Revolutionary War to Desert Storm, more than 3 million men and women made the ultimate sacrifice by giving their lives because they believed our country and the values it stands for were worth it. Like these, we too find ourselves in a war today. It is not a war of guns and bombs, but a profound cultural war. Its casualties are our children. If we are to win this cultural war, we must become the "salt and light" in the political arena. We must be willing to make the required sacrifice. If 3 million people could die to preserve this nation, certainly we can live to do the same.

America's Future Hangs in the Balance

Today, the future of America hangs in the balance. It is up to you and me—the Christians throughout this great nation—to get on our knees and pray, educate ourselves, and mobilize the members of our churches to action. Our nation's future is at stake. The challenge stands before us. The question each of us must answer is this: Will I accept this challenge?

As you search your heart for the answer to that question, let me give you a quote to think about. Edmund Burke, British statesman and orator in the 1700s, said, "The only thing necessary for the triumph of evil is for good men to do nothing."[6]

Christians can change our country. Every day I talk to reporters who look to groups like Concerned Women for America for an opposing viewpoint—a different solution from what the world is holding up—on many of the problems discussed earlier. You and I have a tremendous opportunity to influence public policy in order to open the doors for the truth of the gospel to be communicated in all areas of our society.

The choice is ours to make. We can either do nothing and answer to the Lord for the consequences of our inaction, or we can join together and work to restore our country to its rightful place as "one nation under God."

Notes

1. Peter Marshall, *The Light and the Glory* (Old Tappan, N. J.: Fleming H. Revell Co., 1977), 309.
2. William V. Wells, *The Life and Public Services of Samuel Adams*, 3 vols. (Boston: Little, Brown & Co., 1865).
3. J. Eidsmoe, *Christianity and the Constitution: The Faith of Our Founding Fathers* (Grand Rapids: Baker Book House, 1987), 13.
4. Benjamin Hart, *Faith & Freedom: The Christian Roots of American Liberty* (San Bernardino, Calif.: Here's Life Publishers, 1988), 18.
5. Tim LaHaye, *Faith of Our Founding Fathers* (Wolgemuth & Hyatt Publishers, 1987), 194.
6. John Bartlett, *Bartlett's Familiar Quotations* (Toronto: Little, Brown & Co. Limited, 1980), 374.

11

How Christians Can Make a Difference from Within the Government

By H. Robert Showers, Jr.

Christians can make a difference in the political process, but it depends on their perception of what they want to do and what is true.

Bill Hybels, pastor of the Willow Creek Church in Chicago, speaks of impact players and asks: What is it that the college recruiters and pro recruiters are looking for? What are they looking for when they are going to the first round to draft their first person? Are they looking for the good player? Are they looking for someone who has a lot of talent? Are they looking for recruits who come into the game and change the way the game is played and the outcome? He says they are looking for players who make a difference—impact players. That's what God wants of us. He wants us to be impact players. He wants us in everything that we do to be prepared to have the wall built in such a way that when He calls us onto the stage we can be impact players.

I moved to Washington about six years ago and began asking, "What is it in this town and in the capitals around our country that we can do to make an impact in government?" I have heard two answers. The first comes from the secular society. It says if you want to make a difference, first look at motive, method, and then goal. The motive, they said, is that you are looking for power, prestige, and position because that's how you're going to get something done. The method is very clear. You use your brain. You manipulate, and you use deception. You are ruthless in what you do, and you are overpowering. That's how you make a difference. The goal is very simple too. It is personal gain through whatever you can accomplish. It is rising in the ranks. That is what it's all about here, and that's what it is all about in most of the state capitals and government entities. That's how they "make a difference."

The second answer is found in 2 Corinthians 5:17: "Therefore if any man be in Christ, he is a new creature: old things are passed away; behold, all things are become new." I am learning, and I have learned the new ways. I had to unlearn the old ways, which I learned in college, law school, and my career. I had to unlearn them so I could become an impact player for the Lord. As I became a new creature in Christ, I learned I must make a difference for God and His Kingdom, not for myself in order to get my position and power. The method must be according to His Word—truthfulness, straightforwardness, humility, meekness. And the goals must be for God's purpose and His glory.

As a new creature looking back over the past 10 years of what God has allowed me to do, I want to share four ways I believe Christians can be impact players.

How do you become an impact player? I moved to Washington to be Special Assistant to the Attorney General, heading up the Criminal Justice area. I am here because of God. I had none of the credentials; I knew none of the people. I feel as if they picked me out of a computer and said, "This person happens to be the one that we want for this position." I was too young. I hadn't done enough. I was not in the Washington scene. I didn't have parents or relatives in the political circles. I didn't have any real political connections.

When I arrived, I was situated next to a person who two years before had been at the White House. He was also the man who asked me to head up the Attorney General's Commission on Pornography. At the time, it was called the President's Commission on Pornography, but it ended up being the Attorney General's Commission on Pornography. I told my new mentor that I believed God had called me to D.C., and I wanted to make a difference. This man told me something I shall long remember: "You can do anything in Washington if you give someone else the credit and take none of the credit for yourself." I have found that to be true. If you take none of the credit and give everyone else the credit, you win.

Humility Was First Lesson

He was talking about humility. Humility was my first lesson. James 4:6-10 and 1 Peter 5:5-9 offer the same message: "But he giveth more grace. Wherefore he saith, God resisteth the proud, but giveth grace unto the humble. Submit yourselves therefore to God. Resist the devil, and he will flee from you. . . . Humble yourselves in the sight of the Lord, and he shall lift you up" (Jas. 4:6-7, 10). "Be clothed with humility: for God resisteth the proud, and giveth grace to the humble. Humble yourselves therefore under the mighty hand of God, that he may exalt you in due time: . . .your adversary the devil, as a roaring lion, walketh about, seeking whom he may devour: Whom resist stedfast in the faith" (1 Pet. 5:5-6, 8-9). Those verses spoke to me. They talked about pride. They talked about Satan and how Satan uses pride.

At the Pornography Commission, I quickly learned to give credit to everyone else, take none of it for myself, and devise a strategy.

When I arrived, the Attorney General had assigned the Pornography Report to his Assistant Attorney General and special assistants. They had a group overseeing the report. After I was there about a month, the group voted 9 to 3 to shelve the report. I knew that was not what God wanted. Two other believers and I set out to change that decision. We fasted and prayed about the matter. We went to each assistant attorneys general to share what each of us had learned about the harm of pornography, about what it did to individuals and families in our country. We asked them to reconsider. A month later we voted 11 to 1 to recommend to the Attorney General the creation of a national task force to do everything possible to stop pornography. God authored that turnaround. We were merely the vessels He used.

Obey God, Not People

Second, I learned to obey God and not man. In Romans 16:19-20, it says, "For the report of your obedience has reached to all; therefore I am rejoicing over you, but I want you to be wise in what is good, and innocent in what is evil, and the God of peace will soon crush Satan under your feet." That sounds easy, but it's not. How do you rise in government? Psalm 24:1-7 says:

> The earth is the Lord's, and the fullness thereof; the world, and they that dwell therein. For he hath founded it upon the seas, and established it upon the floods. Who shall ascend into the hill of the Lord? or who shall stand in his holy place? He that hath clean hands, and a pure heart; who hath not lifted up his soul unto vanity, nor sworn deceitfully. He shall receive the blessing from the Lord, and right-eousness from the God of his salvation. This is the generation of them that seek him, that seek thy face, O Jacob. Lift up your heads, O ye gates; and be ye lift up, ye everlasting doors; and the King of glory shall come in.

The first part of this passage is about receiving a blessing by having clean hands and not swearing by what is false, but by being truthful. Lifting up the gates became clear to me when I understood what occurred in the Old Testament times. The author is referring to gates on city walls. A person's rank in the Kingdom would determine how high the gates were lifted for that person to enter the city. For instance, when the king came in, the gates were lifted all the way to the top. That is why the Bible says lift up the gates, so the King of glory may come in. That spoke to my heart because there are places in our lives that God wants to enter, but we must first lift up the gates. We talk about our lives as houses in which Christ can enter. We often won't let Him into every room, or as these verses say, we won't open all the gates to Him. We will give Him the living room, but He doesn't get the bedroom. We're certainly not going to give Him the kitchen. That's very similar.

There were five gates God showed me that I needed to lift up in my life if I was to obey Him and not people. I needed to lift up the ear gate. The key to lifting up that ear gate was through listening. I needed to hear what God was saying to me. There are 28 domestic satellites out there, each having 12 to 24 transponders. Unless you have a power source, an antenna, and a tuner, you won't hear them. God saturates our world, too. He is trying to speak to us through His Word and through His Holy Spirit. Because we do not listen and do not tune in, we do not understand the power source. We don't understand that we need an antenna and a tuner, and we don't hear what He is trying to say to us. We don't lift up that gate.

Heart Gate Opens With Thankfulness

The second gate is the heart gate. The key to opening the heart gate is thankfulness. The greatest enemy of thankfulness is expectations.

The third area is the mind gate, referring to how we obey God. This was the hardest one for me. I'm still struggling with this one.

The key to the mind gate is teachableness. I am perhaps in the process of becoming teachable. Proverbs 12:1 challenges me. It says whoever loves discipline loves knowledge, but whoever hates reproof is stupid. I didn't know "stupid" was in the Bible until I read the New International Version. I certainly didn't know it applied to me because I certainly didn't love discipline. I read Hebrews 12:5-8 which said, "My son do not regard lightly the discipline of the Lord, nor faint when you are reproved by him, for those whom the Lord loves he disciplines, and he scourges every son whom he receives." Whoever doesn't have discipline, "you are illegitimate children and not sons." I needed to be teachable, and I believe every one of us should be teachable.

The fourth area is the soul gate—humility. What can hinder God's perfect will in our lives? Joseph, the Old Testament patriarch, is a good example of that. What his brothers meant for evil, God turned to good. Can circumstances hinder it? Romans 8:28 clearly says that's not true because "all things work together for good to them that love God, to them who are the called according to his purpose." We have to love the Lord to be called according to His purpose. There is nothing passive about that verse. Clearly, circumstances can't hinder the will of God. What can defeat the will of God? Pride! The soul gate, the key to opening that, is humility.

Fifth, the body gate, and this is the one I have dealt with in the drug, pornography, and sexual abuse arenas. This is the one where both our country and churches fall. The key to the body gate is holiness. Two sins persist inside the body gate. "Be holy and I am holy," the Bible says in 1 Peter 1:16. The destruction of church and political leaders through sexual sin or greed is being played out almost every day in the newspapers. All we have to do is look in the newspapers and see the politicians, the great business leaders, and the church leaders brought down by sexual sin.

In working with a national psychiatric institute that ministers to Christians, primarily pastors and lay leaders, an internal survey found that 35 percent of the pastors and priests they work with consume and use pornography, and 25 percent of those in the study are involved in sexual immorality. If those figures are even partially true—and I believe those figures are very close—there is tremendous sexual sin in our churches. It is silent. It is deadly. It will kill every time.

I recently ministered to a large Baptist church in our part of the country. The pastor walked away from his wife of 25 years, acknowledged a relationship with his secretary, and resigned from the church.

In 1 Thessalonians 4:3 it says, "For this is the will of God, even your sanctification, that ye should abstain from fornication." Holiness is tied very closely with sexual morality.

The third area is pleasing God and not people. But I have learned that I am a people-pleaser, not a God-pleaser. That is not what is going to make us effective impact players. Until we want to please God we will not make an impact because we will always go the way that people will take us. We will always want the praise and slap on the back from other people.

First Thessalonians 2:4 says, "But as we were allowed of God to be put in trust with the gospel, even so we speak; not as pleasing men, but God, which trieth our hearts." It is impossible to please God without faith. If we want to be God-pleasers, then all we have to do is read Hebrews 12, the "Hall of Fame of the Faithful," because it is impossible to please God without faith.

Trust God When Nothing Seems Possible

North Carolina, my home state, was said about six years ago to be number one in pornographic outlets per capita. We had tried to change the law for 10 years. We had had a system of government that was not going to allow this situation to change. People and pastors in our state said, "Nothing can be done about this situation." However, there were a few people who said, "I believe God wants it to be done." These people said, "It will be so according to God not people." Within a year this group spearheaded a move to rewrite the entire North Carolina

Child Protection and Obscenity Enforcement Act of 1985. Soon thereafter South Carolina followed suit and adopted the North Carolina law verbatim. It has now been adopted verbatim in 7 states, and 17 other states have adapted it. It was the model state legislation for the Attorney General's Commission on Pornography. It all began because someone wanted to please God rather than people.

Two years later Congress wrote the Child Protection and Obscenity Enforcement Act of 1988, which rewrote almost all of the laws on obscenity and child pornography for the federal government. The bill passed on the last day of 1988, at the last hour and the last minute. It was the last bill to pass, and it passed because some people had the eyes of faith. I drafted that bill and did so despite the objections of many people because I believed it was right in the sight of God.

How do you become an impact player? By humility, obeying God not people, pleasing God not people, and having an eternal purpose.

We Can't Choose Wrong

In the 1850s Abraham Lincoln was in a debate with Stephen Douglas. Douglas was very well-spoken and gave the virtues of why it was important to give the slaveholders a choice whether to keep slaves or not. He made an eloquent argument and convinced everyone in the crowds. It was reported that Lincoln stood up, looked at the audience, and said, "You never have the right to be able to choose wrong."

That is an eternal perspective. *Choice* is the great word today. We have the right to choose to kill infants. We have the right to choose to exploit women and children through pornography. We have the right to choose to do all kinds of things with illegal drugs. We should never stand for something we know is absolutely, categorically wrong and leads not to the Kingdom of God but to the kingdom of Satan. We have to stand in the gap. He is calling us to stand in the gap.

Some people dream of great accomplishments while others stay awake and do them.

127

12

How Christians Can Have an Impact as Volunteers

By Jay Strack

Our nation is suffering from a conflict of visions. We've heard phrases, and sometimes facetiously, "the good guys versus the bad guys," "our side versus their side," "Republican versus Democrat," but I think it really transcends all of that and boils down to just one issue: a conflict of vision. The Bible says that without vision the people perish, but I want to remind you that without people the vision will perish. Without exception, if we are to be leaders, and if we are to win this conflict of vision, we had best motivate other people to be involved and serve.

In thinking about this conflict of vision, first of all, if we Christians are to make a difference in this arena of social issues, we must decide what issues we are going to emphasize. All of us have different issues that motivate us.

Abortion is one of those central issues for me. I am very, very grateful that my wife is very active in the crisis pregnancy center that our church sponsors. I'm very grateful that we have learned the difference between just being against abortion and being pro-life. There's more to it than just being against abortion. I have noticed that some people speak about abortion in such a way that those who have ever had an abortion may not ever be reached with the gospel of Jesus Christ. You can be against abortion and believe it is the taking of human life, but I believe you can do it in such a way that those who have had an abortion will come up after you get through speaking and with tears streaming down their faces say, "Is there any way God can forgive me? Does God still love me?" One of the things that motivates me is when I see young women who, after they receive Jesus as their Lord and Savior, do not have a planned abortion and look to the church and God's people for help.

Being Pro-Life More Than Preaching

When I was pastor of Riverside Baptist Church in Ft. Myers, Florida, I learned that it was one thing to preach against abortion, but it was another thing to be pro-life. I watched as we joined hands with some other denominations and came up with a home for unwed mothers—not just a crisis pregnancy center, but a home. We had several hundred people in our church volunteer to help in the home. I didn't know what to do with them. I wasn't ready for that response, but soon we had doctors and nurses who for free would counsel those young women. We had dentists who would take care of their teeth. We had folks who opened their homes, gave them jobs, provided clothes, went and fixed up a house, and paid for it. Then we found out many of these young women were not finishing high school because of their situation, so we developed a place (in Lee County, Florida) called LAMP—Lee Adolescent Mothers Program. They met at our church. We provided the facilities for free.

Folks found out that we were not only against abortion, but that we were pro-life and would help these young women to be able to finish their education. We had health classes in our church for those pregnant mothers, and as often as we could we got counseling for the young men who were the fathers. We talked to them about options they had and their choices. So through our ministry, I have seen what happens when God's people are willing to get involved and make a difference.

When we talk about the conflict of visions, we need to examine our own visions. Three types of visions will determine what kind of volunteer and what kind of servant we will be for the cause of Christ.

First, there is our vision of the Lord himself. I never cease to be amazed at how people have different concepts of the Lord Jesus Christ. What is your vision of Jesus? What is your vision of the Lord? I believe our God is an awesome God. That's a very popular song today and is sung in many churches and gets a lot of air time on Christian radio stations. Our God is an awesome God. Some generations might say our God is a groovy God, but say what you want, you need to know that this God whom we preach about, this God whom we sing about, this God whom we talk about is, indeed, an awesome God. In fact, there are several theological truths that, if you hold these truths dear, I believe they will transform your life. Do you believe God can do it? What is your vision of Jesus Christ? Is our God a mighty God, an awesome God, an everlasting God? Did our God create this world? Did our God raise the dead? Did our God judge this rebellious little planet and spare a family? Did our God create a nation called Israel and do miracle after miracle?

One of the most tragic verses that describes our generation is found in Psalm 44:1 which says, "We have heard with our ears, O God, our fathers have told us, what work thou didst in their days, in the times of old." The rest of that Psalm is a recapitulation of all the mighty acts of God—the Red Sea, plagues, and power from the hand of God. There is not one reference in that psalm to "our eyes have seen." It just simply says, "Our ears have heard what you used to do a long time ago in the days of our fathers."

A Degenerate World: Madonna and Company

We'll never understand why young women are passed around like a pack of cigarettes. We'll never understand why 10 million young people are hiding behind the chemical curtain of alcohol alone. Add to that those using crack, PCP, angel dust, ice, and other forms of cocaine, and we're talking about 15 million of our nation's youth who hide behind the chemical curtain and are drowning in a sea of alcohol. We'll never understand why young people attempt to take their lives and why so many do so. We'll never understand why they get caught up in the mind-bending, Bible-bending cults. It is very simple. This generation has not even heard about the mighty works of God. I was seventeen years old before anybody even shared with me John 3:16. I was seventeen before I ever heard that the surfer's cross I wore around my neck stood for Jesus

130

who died and gave His life for me. Madonna said something that sent a cold chill through me. A reporter asked Madonna why she wears a cross. Why the fixation with the crucifix? Here is what she said: "I believe that the cross is beautiful and why shouldn't I? It has a naked man on it."

To my generation, Jesus was a naked man who hung on the cross. I would like to share with Madonna that "Yes, it is true. There was a naked man who died on the cross, but He died for you. He gave His life for you, and He was buried for you. And guess what? He is not dead anymore. He is alive."

What is your vision of God? What is your vision of Jesus Christ? Is your God a mighty God, an active God, a God of intervention? When you go to the catacombs in Rome, you will see the murals on the wall where those early Christians met. The murals have had to be restored because the early Christians had to use burning torches to see at night. On the walls of the catacombs the early Christians drew Noah's ark, Daniel and the lion's den, the three Hebrew children and the fiery furnace, the Red Sea, Elijah and the fiery chariot, Lazarus coming out of the grave, and Jesus Christ being resurrected. The one thing that motivated those early Christians to withstand the pressure and the tribulations was very simple: Our God is a mighty God. We must believe that God can do it, whether it is cancer that we're battling, a son who has broken our hearts, a daughter who has gone astray, a marriage that needs a miracle, a loved one who needs to be saved, or someone enslaved in homosexuality or entrapped by alcohol or drug addiction, we must believe that God can help them.

Second, you must believe that God can do it through us. One of the most exciting days of my life was when I found out that God wanted to do His work through me. God can use me! God can use you! I am grateful that I am able to speak to almost one million students every fourteen months. I have had a lot of throat trouble for one reason. I sometimes speak five and six times a day in public schools for free about the battle for the mind and alcohol and drugs, following the crowd, suicide, peer pressure, and the battle for the body. I have found out that God can use me. I can't undo the fact that I was involved in drugs, and I can't undo the things in my life that harmed others. I can, by the grace of God, do what I can to make a difference. There are a lot of us with a lot of talent and a lot of ability. What are you doing for the cause of Christ? What are you doing for the cause of righteousness?

God Wants It Done His Way

We have heard some folks say that the bottom line is "Just get the job done," but I am also convinced that God expects us to get the job done His way in His Spirit. There is a plant, a member of the chrysanthemum family, that so robs the soil of nutrition it forbids any other similar plant to grow nearby. When I read about that plant, it reminded me of a lot of folks I know who call themselves Christian. We are willing to do things our way when we want to do it, the way we want it done, and when we get through nothing else seems to be able to grow in that flower bed. I am convinced that when we say God can do it and God can do it through me there is a lot to that. I believe He expects us to do it. I don't believe the scorched-earth policy has ever been Jesus' way.

The third theological truth is that God can do it through me right here where I am right now. When we talk about Christians responding to social issues, we don't have to go to Washington. We don't have to run for Congress.

There are a lot of people who have an erroneous vision of their Lord. Luke 10:38-42 is tragic. This is the story of Mary and Martha. We know the conflict and the tension in that story. It says, "Now it came to pass, as they went, that he entered into a certain village: and a certain woman named Martha received him into her house. And she had a sister called Mary, which also sat at Jesus' feet, and heard his word. But Martha was cumbered about much serving, and came to him, and said, Lord, dost thou not care that my sister hath left me to serve alone? bid her therefore that she help me." Now, if I understand it right, that is an oxymoron. We don't tell the Lord what to do. A disciple of the Lord does what he or she is told to do by Him.

Yes, Christ Is the Answer

The conflict of visions is not just light against darkness. The conflict goes on in our own lives. What is your vision of the Lord? The Bible tells me in Philippians 2 that I am to have this mind in me that Jesus Christ had in Him. Even though He was equal with God, He took upon Himself the lowly form of a servant, and He was obedient even unto death on the cross. Because He humbled Himself, God has "highly exalted Him and given Him a name which is above every name: That at the name of Jesus every knee should bow, . . . and every tongue should confess that Jesus Christ is Lord" (Phil. 2:9-11). I

132

believe with all my heart the vision we have of the Lord Jesus will determine our service.

Also, there is the vision that we have of other people. What is your view or vision of other people? We have already said that without vision the people perish. We have also said that without the people the vision perishes. We have received a vision of the resurrected Savior, Jesus Christ. We say Christ is the answer. That is not a cliche to us. He *is* the answer.

One time I was approached by a homeless person, and he said, "Man, do you have a quarter?"

I said, "No, I don't have a quarter, but if you will walk with me where I'm going, two blocks, I will give you $2.00." I knew I had $2.00 in my pocket. We walked over, and I was able to talk to him about Jesus. I gave him $5.00. Now, I don't always recommend that, but as we walked and talked, here is what blessed me. I gave him a card, and I said, "Just remember that there is somebody in Dallas who is going to be praying for you." Later, I received a scribbled note at the hotel where I was staying. It read, "You're only the second person to tell me that Jesus loves me, and it reminded me of what my mama taught me. Pray for me. I don't want to live like I'm living." Now that is a small example, $5.00. How do we view other people? Who are those people? Are they dirty? Are they homeless? Are they an annoyance?

Jesus Defines Who Is Our Neighbor

Think about the parable of the good Samaritan. Jesus, in Luke 10:30, answers the question, "Who is my neighbor?"

> And Jesus answering said: "A certain man went down from Jerusalem to Jericho, and fell among thieves, which stripped him of his raiment, and wounded him, and departed, leaving him half dead. And by chance there came down a certain priest that way: and when he saw him, he passed by on the other side. And likewise a Levite, when he was at the place, came and looked on him, and passed by on the other side. But a certain Samaritan, as he journeyed, came where he was: and when he saw him, he had compassion on him, And went to him, and bound up his wounds, pouring in oil and wine, and set him on his own beast, and brought him to an inn, and took care of him."

Then Jesus said, "So which of these three do you think was neighbor to him who fell among the thieves?"

133

We all know this story. It was the highway of blood, and when the work on the temple had been completed thousands of people were unemployed. Craftsmen, masons, and laborers were unemployed. Many of them lived in the Judean wilderness in the caves, waiting for people to go to the Miami Beach of Israel, which was Jericho. Herod had his winter palace there. The Scripture says he went down from Jerusalem to Jericho (the highway of blood, Jerome called it), and he fell among the thieves, and he was left for dead. In this parable not only do I see a vision of the Lord—a good Samaritan to me is a picture of Jesus Christ. I don't know what visions others have of the Lord, but that is my vision of the Lord Jesus.

Notice the different ways that folks look at people. Here is what I am afraid is happening in the Christian world. I am afraid this conflict of vision is not light against darkness. I am afraid that with some of us it has been so long since we have had the tears of Jesus that our own vision has become cloudy, and our own vision lacks perception.

Some viewed people as objects. Those who robbed this man looked on another human being and said, "This man is just an object. He exists for me. What he has I want. I am entitled to what belongs to him, and I will take what I want when I want it." Remember, there are those who call themselves human beings who use other people. They see people as objects.

Then the Bible tells us there were those who passed by and saw the man lying in the ditch--well-educated people, successful people, religious leaders. The Bible says when they saw the man in the condition he was in, they went to the other side of the road and went on their way. There are some people who see people as obstacles. "I don't have time to be involved with you. I don't have time for your problems, for your needs. I don't have time to get involved in your life."

Many of us are involved in many aspects of various ministries. Do we see people as objects? I have noticed that some people like some people as long as they do just what they want them to do. I am convinced that most churches want a puppet instead of a prophet. They want to be able to pull a person's strings. Then when they get a prophet, they don't know what to do with him or her.

The last conflict of vision is our vision of ourselves. The Bible tells me that to be a follower of Jesus Christ I must be a servant. That word translated *servant* in the New Testament is an interesting word, but to be honest, it is not a pretty word. It is the word for "lower row." It is the word used to describe someone on a slave galley ship, and those who were on the lowest rung in the bottom of that boat.

A Generation of Peacocks

We have a generation of peacocks who want to serve Jesus Christ. I have found that peacocks one day are feather dusters the next. God has a way of humbling people. Are you a lower rower? What is your vision of yourself? Am I too good to volunteer? Am I too good and too busy to make a visit? Am I too important to stop and talk to someone on the street?

I had the opportunity to speak on Sally Jessy Raphael's show. The subject was homosexuality. When I got through speaking, a guy walked up to me and said, "I have AIDS."

I said, "Man, I'm sorry."

He said, "What do you think about that?"

I said, "I think you need to get saved real quick."

He said, "Would Jesus even want me?" We talked 10 minutes. He didn't think Jesus wanted him.

I said, "Can I pray for you?" He said yes and I did. Some people standing nearby made cat calls. When I got through praying with him, I gave him a hug. I said, "I'm going to be praying for you, man."

I hadn't walked 15 feet when he said, "I think Jesus does love me. Would you pray that I might be saved?" Now, I don't run around telling everybody to hug folks who have AIDS, but I'll tell you this, when Jesus Christ tells you to do something, He will take care of you. Jesus told me to hug that AIDS victim and I did. I did because I believe that is what Jesus would have done.

When the Special Olympics took place in San Antonio, it captured the heart of this nation. Some of those young men and women had worked and trained for years to fulfill their dream to be in the Special Olympics. Some of them may have had more significant handicaps than others. Some of them were tall and lanky, and some were very short and squatty. Some were very coordinated, and others couldn't get everything to work just when it was supposed to. At the sound of the gun, they took off for the finals of the 440-yard race, for the Gold Medal in the Special Olympics. Several of them led the way, separated from the pack. The three leaders stopped about 10 feet before reaching the finish line, turned around, and started motioning to all the other runners. "You can do it. Don't quit.

Come on." Finally, they crossed the finish line hand-in-hand together.

You want to know how Christian volunteers can change their society? We can register folks to vote, and I have been involved in a lot of that through the years. We can be politically active. We ought to be; it is a sin not to be. We can give. We can vote. We can orchestrate. We can hand out leaflets. We can fight. We can defend. To me a Christian volunteer is someone who knows, by the grace of God, that "I'm going to cross the finish line. I just don't want to cross it by myself. I want to take someone with me."